BRAIN GAMES FOR PUPPIES

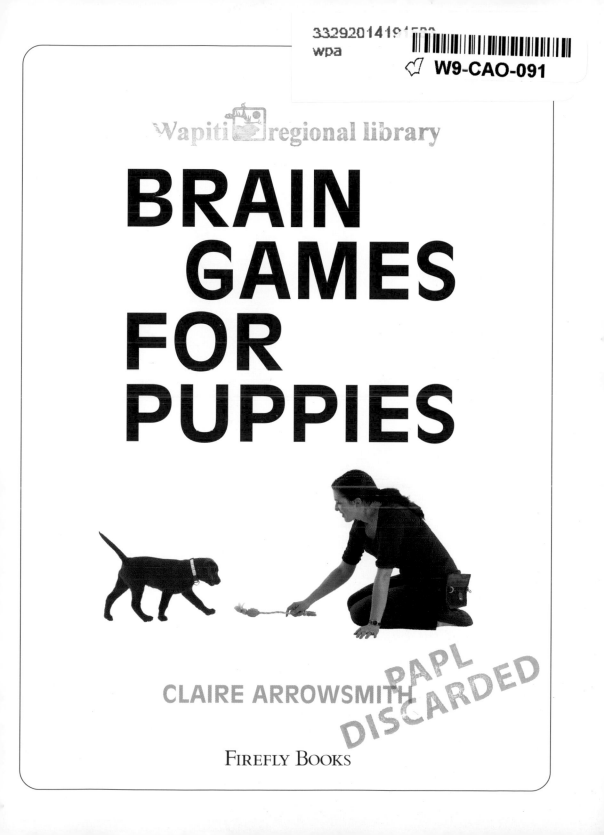

CLAIRE ARROWSMITH

FIREFLY BOOKS

A FIREFLY BOOK

Published by Firefly Books Ltd. 2014

First printing

Publisher Cataloging-in-Publication Data (U.S.)

CIP data for this title can be obtained from the Library of Congress

Library and Archives Canada Cataloguing in Publication

Arrowsmith, Claire, author
    Brain games for puppies / Claire Arrowsmith.
ISBN 978-1-77085-401-7 (pbk.)
    1. Games for dogs. 2. Puppies—Training.
I. Title.
SF427.45.A773 2014   636.7'0887   C2014-900613-6

Published in the United States by
Firefly Books (U.S.) Inc.
P.O. Box 1338, Ellicott Station
Buffalo, New York 14205

Published in Canada by
Firefly Books Ltd.
50 Staples Avenue, Unit 1
Richmond Hill, Ontario L4B 0A7

Printed in China by 1010 Printing

Conceived, designed, and produced by Interpet Publishing, Vincent Lane, Dorking, Surrey RH4 3YX, England. **Editor** Philip de Ste. Croix; **Designer** Philip Clucas MCDS; **Photographer** Roddy Paine; **Production management** Consortium, Suffolk

CHAPTER ONE

The Benefits of Puppy Play

CONTENTS

CONTENTS continued overleaf ▶

With a little ingenuity, ordinary items around the home can become props for a brain game.

Author's Note
Brain Games are meant to be played by all puppies, but I have chosen to describe them as male throughout the game descriptions. This is purely to simplify the text and does not mean to imply that the games are not suitable for female puppies.

Party games build on the basics of obedience training to develop into smart tricks.

PART ONE

INTRODUCTION
THREE CHEERS FOR PUPPIES!

Dogs are very popular household companions — it is estimated that over half of all households in the U.S. own dogs. This accounts for more than 90 million dogs in these parts of the world alone. Although all these puppies sprang from different backgrounds and many have different roles to play, I am sure that most owners hope that the puppies that we bring into our lives will remain our lifelong companions. Often they become as attached to us as human family members.

PARTNERSHIP
Dogs have not become this in-volved in our lives by accident. His-torically there were significant advan-tages in living and working together for mutual benefit. Over thousands of years dogs have evolved to become superbly suited to our many different lifestyles, and it would be hard to visualize a world without them.

Aside from the working aspect of dogs, we must also recognize that living with a dog brings emotional and physical benefits to humans too. Dog ownership encourages adults and children to be more active, and it has been linked with lower cholesterol and blood pressure levels. Dog ownership can reduce the severity of anxiety disorders and has been shown to increase positive social contact for humans with various forms of physical or sensory impairment. Over recent years, exciting research has shown that dogs can detect by smell and alert us to very early signs of cancer and other conditions including diabetes and seizures. Dogs too have benefited from increasingly improved health care and diet, and owners will go to incredible lengths to ensure their pet has the best of everything with a dizzying array of products available for all income levels.

MUTUAL BENEFITS

It pays to maximize your relationship with your puppy in order to improve its health, reduce training and socialization issues and to keep the puppy as happy and stimulated as possible. By doing this, behavioral problems should be reduced and, if they do crop up, the puppy/owner bond should be strong enough to remain positive through a behavior modification program. I firmly believe that having fun with your puppy and playing *Brain Games* is part of a healthy owner–dog relationship. I hope that after reading this book, you will agree with me.

Puppies are remarkably adaptable. The family ties that they feel for their canine mother are naturally strong and present from birth. But a puppy entering a human household will swiftly integrate himself into the new family dynamic and grow to become a much-loved member of the home. The puppy benefits, and so do the owners. It is the perfect win-win situation.

THE BENEFITS OF PUPPY PLAY

Play: (to) engage in (a game or activity)
for enjoyment.
Game: an activity that one engages in for
amusement.
The Oxford English Dictionary

While the concept of play may appear frivolous and something that we assume is only for "young" individuals, it actually fulfills a vital role in the development of other important life skills. Play can involve complex interaction and varies according to different situations. It allows a young member of a species to practice and develop actions that will be important as an adult when there may be no time for such practice and when behavior patterns are less flexible.

Just as we see young children learning through exploration and social feedback, puppies rely

> **PLAY CAN BENEFIT
> YOUR RELATIONSHIP**
> Any activity that promotes positive emotional reactions will also benefit your (and your puppy's) overall mental health. This, in turn, benefits physical health too. Extra play activity is also a great way to increase exercise levels which, of course, improves good health.

LEFT Puppies must learn while still young that biting their owner's hands is not acceptable behavior.

on having the opportunity to learn about what is and what is not appropriate behavior. Therefore, brain games should not be considered as an activity just for owners who

are dog-obsessed; rather they can benefit all types of dogs, and the result of playing brain games may be the difference between a manageable dog and a problem one.

Early play is important Learning in young animals happens swiftly, sometimes after only one event. This is partly because they lack prior experience or expectations, and partly because they have extremely receptive young brains. It is also safe since they don't possess the strength or physical weapons to cause severe injury. Although your puppy's teeth are needle sharp, they cause less damage than adult teeth growing in jaws that are driven by far greater muscle power. So it is very important that your puppy learns how to control his bite while young and how to behave appropriately before he grows bigger and stronger.

PREVENTING FUTURE BEHAVIORAL PROBLEMS

Behavior problems commonly develop over time, or are triggered by specific events in the puppy's life. It is possible to minimize the risk of future problems by ensuring that your puppy comes from the best genetic stock, enjoys a thorough period of socialization and a good level of training (using pain-free methods). However, until there

RIGHT The act of playing with a young puppy is a hugely pleasurable experience. It's fun to do, and helps to build a loving bond between you. It also enables the puppy to learn about the world in a controlled way.

Little treats are always popular.

is a recognized problem the prospect of "preventing" an issue may not seem that important. Certainly, most problem behaviors are only recognized once they have become established and have breached the owner's perception of what is tolerable and "normal" puppy behavior.

Brain games aim to create fun interactions between you and your puppy that help you to naturally promote desirable life skills, creating a good framework for the future. Play naturally provides physical and mental stimulation and an appropriate platform for your puppy to develop and fine-tune his emotional responses. Through play your puppy can also learn improved physical control and begin to appreciate boundaries. **Play is rarely seen in animals experiencing psychological stress or those with physical problems, although how much play behavior is lost depends on the condition**.

Of course, play is not the cure for all behavioral difficulties. Some dogs have never learned to control their impulses while others suffer from excessive fear. Those problems need to be addressed by a professional. Adding more stimulation to the life of a dog that already cannot cope is not an automatic solution. However, the provision of stimulation is generally a healthy approach to take.

LEFT Play with toys allows a puppy to express natural behaviors harmlessly in the home.

9

THE PUPPY BRAIN AND SENSES

Your puppy has amazing potential. This is true of any dog of any breed. Of course, it takes a special dog to warn their owner of a pending seizure, or to successfully search a mountain or disaster scene for casualties, but every dog has the potential to inspire us and do amazing things. We don't have the ability to see the world in the way a puppy does as we don't have the

ABOVE Puppies have an insatiable curiosity about the world around them, and are keen to investigate new experiences.

appropriate sensory system, but even a tiny puppy is incredible. Like us, he takes in information about the world via his senses of smell, hearing, sight, touch and taste. These senses are so acute that the world must appear very different in the puppy's perception. We can hardly imagine what a

puppy experiences every day. His nose has up to 220 million scent receptors compared to our five million and he hears noises up to 60,000Hz in frequency while we may strain to hear 20,000Hz. His highly specialized eyes can also detect movement with more accuracy than we can.

Although your puppy will have particular inherited talents, it quite possible to improve his skills through practice. Certainly, the more the young brain is stimulated and used, the better it will become equipped to deal with the information that the puppy will face at a later date.

WHAT INFLUENCES YOUR PUPPY'S BEHAVIOR?

Your puppy is born with some innate behaviors which are genetically pre-programmed at birth. He will require no practice or learning in order to perform these, although some may not become apparent until later life stages. The remainder of your puppy's behavior develops and is influenced by the experiences he has and is constantly evolving throughout his life although by adulthood his personality type will be fairly stable.

RIGHT A puppy's senses of smell, sight and hearing are very acute.

BELOW Every puppy soon learns that life is full of surprises! Successful training helps a dog to take such things in his stride.

How your puppy learns

As amazing as your puppy is, he is not born knowing how to respond to all the things that life will throw at him, and certainly not with an understanding of human rules. Unfortunately the concept that a puppy or dog should just "behave" or "know it's done wrong" still prevails, but unless we spend time teaching what behaviors we expect, your puppy is bound to continue to make mistakes.

While there is no need for owners to delve into the details of canine learning theory, an understanding of the basic principles will help you make appropriate decisions when teaching your puppy brain games or training obedience.

HABITUATION

This is the most simple form of learning. When your puppy is exposed to something, for example an object, which has little significance for him, he will begin to learn not to respond to it. This has advantages as he can then focus his energies on events that actually matter to him and avoid unnecessary flight or fight reactions. We humans also habituate to our surroundings which allows us to ignore sounds like the ongoing hum of traffic outside. Without sufficient opportunity to habituate to his environment, your puppy is likely to exhibit startle and fear responses as an adult, which may impact on his ability to cope with certain environments.

LEFT Habituation helps a puppy to accept unfamiliar objects without feeling unduly fearful or stressed.

CONDITIONING

This term implies that experiences have created associations (either positive or negative) which continue to influence the emotional and physical responses of an individual, in this case your puppy.

Classical conditioning is all about associations or the pairing up of events and is the technique that the famous Russian scientist Ivan Pavlov studied. By pairing a neutral event with the arrival of a reward (or unpleasant experience), you can strongly influence your puppy's response to the initial event. For instance, if every time a visitor arrives they offer your puppy a reward, he will begin

LEFT Rewards help to shape behavior.

to anticipate this action every time someone comes to the door and will therefore feel positive about the event.

Operant conditioning is about consequences or what happens after your puppy performs a specific action and it will influence whether he repeats it again. For instance, you call your puppy to you and when he arrives, you offer him a treat. He learns that the action of coming back results in pleasure and so is more likely to choose to do this again.

Observational learning occurs when your puppy watches another dog or human and then learns from their actions. Many people hope an older dog will help to train their puppy and to some extent this will happen, although depending on age and character, some unwanted behaviors could begin to rub off on your other dog, so management will always be necessary.

Latent learning occurs without any external sign. This is when your puppy processes information but does not need to perform or practice it until a later date, when that action is needed.

How to use these processes to benefit your brain games. In day-to-day routines you should remember that your puppy learns via the feedback he receives upon performing an action. If the experience is a positive one, he will be more inclined to repeat that action, but if the experience is not so pleasant, he will be less inclined. Generally if you want your puppy to perform in a certain way, you must reward him and teach him to enjoy that activity.

SENSITIVE PERIODS AND SOCIALIZATION

The early weeks and months of a puppy's life have been the focus of many research studies seeking to ascertain the impact of early experience, or the lack of it, on future behavior. Scientists are certain that there is a

Start to play interactive games from an early age.

sensitive period of development between the 3- and 12-week stage during which a puppy is particularly sensitive to new experiences and is generally able to respond to novelty in a positive, inquisitive manner. After this time, although learning certainly does continue, the puppy is less able to accept novelty without also feeling apprehensive (or even fearful). Thus the early weeks are particularly important for the development of social skills. For this reason, under-socialized puppies are more vulnerable to being unable to cope if unexpected events occur or if their lifestyle or environment changes at some point in their lives.

Playing games exposes your puppy to a world of new sights, sounds and activities, allowing a greater range of socialization experiences (people doing different things) and greater comfort with a range of unfamiliar objects. In this way it can help to promote a more robust and confident character as your puppy matures.

Your role begins now! Since most of us would like to own a confident, social puppy that can go out in public, it is advisable to put in valuable time ensuring that your puppy has an excellent socialization while you can. Remember, you can never rewind and take another shot. This is a one-time opportunity so don't waste it!

LEFT A dog that enjoys play is usually a happy dog.

PLANNING YOUR PUPPY'S BRAIN

WHEN CAN A PUPPY BEGIN TO PLAY?

Despite displaying clumsy movements and little coordination, at 3 weeks of age a puppy will be starting to exhibit play behaviors. The type of behavior is guided by their physical abilities and so at first they simply paw at one another and, as their strength and coordina-

BELOW Tussles and "fights" are typical play behavior.

tion come together, they begin to practice jumping, rolling, wrestling, mouthing and chasing. They will also begin to display play behavior toward items such as toys. By the time your puppy is ready to come home to you at around 8 weeks, he should be able to play short, but wonderful, interactive games with you.

Adult dogs' behavior patterns are more "fixed" than those of puppies or young adolescents. When they are very young, actions are easily developed and the puppy is open to the influence of greater amounts of trial and error and exploration. If a puppy is never granted the option of enjoying periods of

play, it is very unlikely that he will ever be able to learn once he has matured and his behavior patterns are less malleable.

Time well spent Although puppies require a lot of sleep to aid their growth and brain development, that still leaves several hours a day where they could potentially find themselves up to mischief. If your puppy's waking hours are occupied doing things that are acceptable to the household, then there will be less opportunity for mistakes to happen and unwanted habits to develop. Your puppy is not born knowing about house rules or which items in the home are yours. He must learn through experience and the direction must come from you.

WHAT GAMES CAN A PUPPY PLAY?

If approached in the right way, your puppy can play a wide variety of games with you as long as his physical needs are always respected and you have realistic expectations about each session. If you think your 9-week-old puppy will be able to master a complex trick first time round, you will inevitably be disappointed. However, if you are prepared to build up the trick in small, manageable parts, then you will be delighted at how quickly he will learn and just how much fun even a young puppy can be.

Two days

GAMES

RIGHT A puppy must learn early that toys are acceptable playthings, but other family possessions usually aren't.

Introduce toys early If your puppy can learn very early on that toys are what you should play with, he will be less inclined to target your possessions or pester your older dog or cat. This simple option is crucial in the prevention of many common puppy problems. If a dog does not learn to play with toys during the early months, it is possible that he may never learn those skills despite your best attempts. A puppy without play is a sad concept to consider.

ARE BRAIN GAMES PHYSICALLY SAFE?

While there are many positive implications of having an active dog, there are also concerns that should be addressed before starting to play games. One of the main worries surrounds the safety of physical exercise and potential damage to a young dog's limbs and joints. While your puppy is growing, the "growth plates" at the ends of his bones remain soft, only hardening once the main growth phase has been completed. It is

thought that this area is particularly susceptible to damage through excessive impact and so hard exercise is not advised, particularly for larger, heavier breeds. However, it is important to understand that controlled exercise is important to build up the muscle that secures your puppy's joints in place, stabilizing movement. It is not healthy or advisable to avoid all exercise with your puppy. If nothing else, the puppy will miss out on important environmental and social interaction, as well as limiting his training opportunity.

ABOVE The whole family will enjoy playing with a puppy

BELOW Don't overexercise your puppy while he is still growing fast.

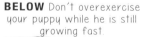

Two weeks

Three weeks

Four weeks

Six weeks

Individual Preferences

No two people are exactly alike. Our genetic code and life experiences will alter the way we interact with and perceive our environment. These factors are also relevant when we consider what games your puppy will like. Don't build up your expectations based upon your previous experiences with another dog in your neighborhood or puppy class. Each dog is different.

It's in the genes There are approximately 300 recognized dog breeds. These have arisen via a lengthy process of selection whereby we have deliberately chosen dogs that possess specific desirable traits and bred them over many generations. By doing this in different parts of the world and to achieve different aims, humans have created this amazing array of breeds. By selecting dogs that were particularly good at certain tasks, we have changed the way they behave as well as altering their physical appearance.

The process of domestication has altered the dog so that it can live alongside humans without excessive risk to us. Studies have shown that the domesticated dog is

TAKE CARE

The size of your puppy is relevant when considering the safety of any activity. Large and giant breeds are more susceptible to injury due to their longer growth period and the sheer weight impacting on their young joints.

less independent and has more advanced social cognition than its wild relatives. Depending on the breed of dog, the impact of domestication may vary, with some of the more "primitive" types, such as the Siberian Husky or Japanese Akita, being less inclined to make eye contact than those breeds created for a purpose where more direct interaction with humans was necessary. This can influence their desire to participate in certain games, but with the right preparation and consideration, the training goals can still be achieved.

Well designed Your dog's physical shape will influence the types of activities that he enjoys. In many cases the shape comes hand in hand with the types of behavior that come naturally to the breed. For example, the short legs and long nose and ears of the Basset Hound make the perfect body shape for following scents and the extra-sensitive olfactory system in that breed makes it perfect it for that purpose. This might have an impact on the types of games that you teach your puppy. Although most of the games described are suitable for all puppies,

RIGHT The next generation at play!

RIGHT Breed type will influence the games a puppy most likes to play

you may have to alter the props used or adjust your expectations to take into account your own puppy's physique and mental acuteness.

AGE INFLUENCE ON BRAIN GAMES

When your puppy first comes home at approximately 8 weeks of age, you will need to focus on brief, fun training sessions of approximately one to two minutes each, with frequent resting periods in between. Over the coming months he will be able to focus for longer so your training sessions can start to stretch to around 10 minutes before you require a break; every puppy is different and so the time you actually spend playing these games should be personally tailored for your puppy. Bring in variety and ensure that the activity is enjoyable as this is the best way to keep the sessions interesting. As your puppy gets used to learning and performing activities, it will be possible to link

more than one task or action together to form more complex tricks or games.

Do not despair if during adolescence your puppy appears to have forgotten many of the lessons you have spent so long teaching. Changing hormones and social influences will alter his motivations, often causing a reduction in the focus paid to owner requests. Remain consistent; if you make tasks enjoyable, achievable and rewarding, then this challenging stage of development will pass without long-term problems developing.

While the puppy is still very young, limit play sessions to just a minute or two.

TIP

Depending upon the original purpose of your puppy's breed, he may have a particular inclination to chase, retrieve, herd or sniff. By directing those natural instincts into appropriate brain games, you can help to prevent them being expressed in unwanted ways or inappropriate situations.

BRAIN GAMES SHOULD BE FUN

Although the intention is to have fun, sometimes owners and puppies can become frustrated and stressed along the way, and the whole point of playing games together is lost. To minimize this risk, consider these key factors when playing with any puppy or dog.

- **Is this brain game fun?** Is the experience rewarding for your puppy? You should only do things that your puppy can feel comfortable doing. Of course, in some cases this means gradually building up to the final "game" in a way that teaches the puppy to feel happy with it.
- **Does your puppy have a choice?** Without choice you risk making the experience extremely aversive for your

BELOW Puppies need frequent periods of rest, so allow plenty of opportunities for a snooze break.

RIGHT
Puppies love an energetic game of tug o' war.

puppy. Never force him to remain with you, or to perform a specific task if he is uncomfortable. You will achieve much more if he is willing and wants to play.
- **Is the game too long or intensive?** A puppy is unable to concentrate on any one task for more than a few minutes at a

time, especially during the first few months. As they get used to the activity, they will gradually improve but it is important to keep games short at first. He will also tire easily and so it is very important to take regular breaks between any training or play activity so that he doesn't begin to find it stressful. Let him choose something else to do, go and have a drink or out to relieve himself, or just to settle down for a proper rest. Remember that sleep is important for a puppy's brain development so resting is an important part of brain games.
- **Where do you play?** Choosing an appropriate place is important since your puppy should feel relaxed in his surroundings. If he is not, he will be distracted and less able to concentrate. Play away from distractions and certainly away from anything that he finds frightening. An older dog or child may interrupt the game or take control of the toys, so ensure that your puppy has plenty of opportunity to learn without this sort of intrusion.

BELOW If you are a bright, responsive playmate, your puppy will enjoy your company

"Hey, this is fun!"

- **When do you play games?** For best performance you should avoid times when your puppy is tired, full or very distracted. If you want him to focus on a task that requires lots of steadiness and concentration, pick a time when he has had a chance to burn off excess energy first.
- **Are you a good playmate?** Your puppy will respond to your mood, body language and play style, so try to behave in a way that helps your puppy to enjoy himself. Try to avoid bodily movements or

LEFT Scratching may be a way of saying "I don't understand what you want."

gestures that your puppy could interpret as a threat, such as suddenly rushing up to him, leaning over, quickly reaching out or using a loud voice.

- **Can you understand your puppy?** Your puppy is a social animal that has developed a lovely array of signals designed to communicate his emotional state. If you can recognize these, then you will know when he is happy and when he is unsure. Some confusion often occurs when a puppy appears to ignore his owner's training request and instead scratches, sniffs or shakes. This could actually be a displacement activity which indicates some emotional conflict. Avoid reprimanding your puppy and think about how you can make the game easier to understand, or ways to help him relax. He may need to have a break and try again later.
- **Do you enjoy this brain game and time with your puppy?** If the answer is no, then you should take time out to think about what it is that you don't enjoy. Revisit the points above and try to identify any problem areas. Are you expecting too much from yourself or your puppy? Try to remember that the aim is to have fun while bonding with your dog!

REWARD YOUR PUPPY

Why? Many owners wonder why they need to reward their puppy during training, especially when teaching a "game" that should be fun in itself. Look at it this way: your puppy is a living, sentient being that feels pleasure and pain. Therefore, he will always prefer to do things that make him feel good. It is up to us to make sure that the desirable actions we want to teach are those that make him feel best. Research has shown that puppies that are rewarded learn quickly and develop fewer problems than those trained with punitive methods. Until your puppy has

ABOVE Patience is a virtue when it comes to puppy training. Sometimes things will go wrong, but try not to lose your temper — it's not going to help.

LEFT Rewards and praise are the best way to shape your puppy's behavior.

learned all about the game and understands how much fun it is, you should be prepared to praise and encourage all the many steps along the road to success.

Rewarding is not spoiling This is a very important distinction to make. If your puppy is taught that rewards come from performing in a certain way, he is actually earning the "wage." This is very different from being offered lots of food or praise for doing nothing, or for free.

RESPONDING TO MISTAKES

Inevitably, puppies make mistakes. This might happen while you are away from home or while you are trying to train them. Remember that this is a baby animal that does not come pre-programmed with an understanding of what humans expect of him. If blame for a mishap must be apportioned, then the owner must take most of it as the puppy has either been given the opportunity to make the mistake or there has been a communication failure. Instead of getting upset with your puppy, try to consider where you went wrong and how you can arrange things so that your puppy will understand and respond differently the next time that he is placed in that situation.

A place for punishment? It is often argued that you must make sure the puppy knows when he has done wrong. In principle yes, but so many pitfalls arise from using punishment that it really has little place in the training of puppies.

First of all, punishment has to be well timed or there is a very real risk that your puppy will associate your response with something else, or even directly with you, resulting in anxiety or fear in new situations or whenever you try to interact with him. Unless you actually catch your puppy doing something unwanted, this is a bad idea. And even if you do, the best thing is to distract him and direct him to an activity that you do want him to do. If you only tell your puppy what he cannot do, you may find the path to succeeding at the right activity is very long and stressful indeed.

We also have difficulty in measuring how much punishment to use. When dogs interact with each other, their mutual communication is highly refined to allow just the right amount of signal appropriate to the situation. We may display an excessive reaction if the puppy has damaged something we particularly like, if we are already tired or

ABOVE Take care with reprimands — you don't want your puppy to start feeling anxious when he is around you.

stressed, or if we are having other issues with the puppy that have already caused tension. This overreaction will not make sense to your puppy, and he could end up feeling very worried about your apparent inconsistency.

KEEP BRAIN GAMES ENJOYABLE FOR YOUR PUPPY

- Make your request simple and achievable.
- Prevent unwanted behavior by blocking access or restricting movement.
- Always encourage desirable activities.
- Interrupt your puppy just as he thinks about doing something wrong and divert him to something you are happy with.
- Take a break if you feel stressed or are not enjoying yourself.

BELOW Puppies can burn off lots of energy by playing with a rope toy.

LEFT Keep treats small to
begin with, little and often
should be your watchwords.

WHAT TREATS CAN A PUPPY BE FED?

This is an important question. First of all please ensure that your puppy is being fed a good quality, appropriate diet in amounts suitable for his age and size. If you do not do this, you risk creating health problems which would frustrate any attempts to play games. As you can imagine, it is hard to play or focus on enjoyable activities if your energy levels are low or if your digestion is upset.

For basic activities many puppies enjoy being offered pieces of their regular food or kibble. Young dogs respond so well to your interaction with them that this is often a sufficient reward. However, it has been shown that for more complex training, offering higher level food rewards achieves the fastest results.

Start small Your puppy will quickly fill up if you offer anything too big as a reward (he will also have to stop participating in the activity to eat it). Begin with small, fingernail-sized pieces.

Use new food sparingly

A new treat may be hard for your puppy's digestion to cope with, so introduce new foods sparingly to allow him to become accustomed to them. If something appears to upset him, stop offering it.

LEFT Keep treats small to begin with, little and often should be your watchwords.

Variety adds interest Use a selection of different treats to prolong your puppy's interest in the rewards you offer. Early exposure to new foods will influence later preferences, so introducing some variety will help to prevent too much focus on one food type.

Motivation Puppies vary in terms of what works as an incentive. We all recognize that what works to motivate us in one circumstance doesn't necessarily in another as it may depend on the level of effort required. This rule also applies to your puppy. As part of the process of getting to know your puppy, you should spend time learning about his preferences since this will help you to achieve better results in all of your interactions together.

Choosing and using food rewards The range of puppy treats commercially available is huge. You have almost anything you desire but in the end it is what your puppy prefers that counts. Whether you buy treats or make your own, *please avoid* offering human chocolates, candy, cookies, grapes, raisins or nuts as these can all harm your puppy.

Taste preferences will differ between puppies but the more variety your puppy is exposed during the early months, the more diverse his tastes will become. However, do remember: new foods and treats should not be offered in excess. Some puppies are very excited by even the most basic of treats. In this case you do not need to use anything other than their basic kibble for most early training.

Treat grades It can be helpful to understand which treats your puppy views as being the ultimate reward so that you can then have a grading system for easier or harder tasks. Offering your puppy a choice of little treats and observing which he chooses to eat first can give you an indication of preferences. Similarly, take note of any that he is slow to take, refuses or spits out as this also can be helpful. If your puppy is suddenly snatching from your hand or appears very hungry, check that the amount of daily food matches his current age, size and activity level as he may simply be hungry. It is quite normal for growth spurts to impact on your puppy's desire for food.

Take care that any treats offered are suitable for a dog

ABOVE A simple test will identify which treats your puppy finds most attractive. Watch what he goes for from a selection laid out on the floor.

"I know you like this."

RIGHT You should break big treats in smaller bite-size portions.

Toy test All toys are not equal. The most expensive puppy toy may excite only the briefest of games while the discarded packaging triggers hours of fun. While there are some toys that are very popular and certainly better than others, your

BELOW The treat test can also be applied to toys, so that you can establish which are your puppy's favorite playthings.

puppy's individual nature will determine which becomes the favorite.

You will certainly need a range of toys. Spread them out on the floor and allow your puppy to investigate. After a short period of time you will probably notice him selecting one in particular over the others. Repeat this activity a few times to check the result and then remove the favorite toy and repeat again. In this way you can discover which toys your puppy absolutely adores and which he is less keen on. Of course, this method isn't entirely infallible as some toys are better fun when tugged or thrown, while others are enjoyed best when the puppy has lots of energy. However, you will develop an understanding of his basic preferences and you can repeat the exercise by using the toys in different circumstances.

Human contact test While most puppies will invite petting and contact, it is very important to remain aware of how keen your puppy is for this to continue. After all, there is a difference between a puppy approaching to say hello and putting up with several minutes of stroking and cuddling. When your puppy approaches you, try to stroke him for a very short time (15 to 30 seconds) and then stop to see how he responds. If he steps away or begins another activity, then you know

BELOW The ball wins this contest.

that he has had enough. It will be very clear if he wants more strokes, as he will return to you for more contact. This way of "checking in" with your dog should become a habit that you continue to practice throughout his life to maintain good levels of communication.

Response to verbal interaction Unless your puppy has hearing problems, you will find that you spend a lot of time talking to

HOW TO ENCOURAGE PLAY BEHAVIOR

To Do	To Avoid
Using quick, excitable movements.	Rushing up to your puppy, especially when he is distracted or sleeping.
Play-bowing: getting down low to invite interaction.	Trying to force your puppy to play or show interest.
Running away and calling your puppy.	Kissing and cuddling your puppy.
Using a higher, excitable voice and quick words.	Shouting at your puppy or using flat tones of voice.
Starting a game with a toy and praising any interest.	Ignoring signs that your puppy is worried or tired.

BELOW Good body language for a playmate.

him. This is a natural, instinctive form of human communication. Most puppies respond well to excited, higher tones of voice but again this will vary between puppies. Try different ways of talking to see what excites your puppy and gets his attention. Some puppies respond with absolute delight to being spoken to, and this reaction on its own can work well to encourage a lot of activities. However, others are less voice-responsive or are overly sensitive to different tones. This can evoke fear or overexcitement and you should adapt how you choose to communicate to take account of this.

Adapting play style During play interaction there is a very interesting occurrence called "self-handicapping." Just as a father will change his play-wrestling style to suit the age of a young child, a dog will also adapt to suit the individual level of their playmate. When this does not happen, problems usually occur during the game. While playing brain games with your dog, remember that you can adapt the activity and/or your expectations to match your puppy's level of maturity. Doing this keeps the game fun, as you intended.

LEFT Learn from the way puppies play together, so that you adapt your play style to suit your pup's abilities.

Think it through When your puppy has only just started learning new games, you will have to offer lots of help and encouragement. However, it is important to allow the pup enough time to think it over and to try to work out what is wanted before you step in to help. Watch your puppy carefully and provide help before he gives up, and make sure he is rewarded really well for getting it right so that the lesson sticks.

ABOVE AND LEFT Dogs use body language to signal their feelings and intentions to other dogs. Gestures like a play-bow or a raised front leg signify readiness to play.

ABOVE Take new games slowly, one step at a time.

Keep it balanced We all know that it is no fun to play games when you always end up losing, and this observation applies to puppies too. Studies have shown that roles are swapped in successful play and so it is reasonable to expect this to apply this to human–puppy play too. Of course, play is a very complex activity and is certainly not always a 50:50 partnership, but each relationship will differ.

Clear signaling It is very important that dogs know when another is just playing with them since misinterpretation could lead to serious fighting and injury. Therefore, dogs have developed lovely play gestures to make

sure that their intention is clear. When dogs play together, they rely on regular "I'm still playing" signals in order to maintain the playful mood throughout. A good game relies on appropriate signals from both parties. Look out for bent elbows: whether your puppy is bending in a play-bow or raising a front leg, recognize that both are the two most obvious signals of playfulness.

Remember to check in with your puppy during play Owners often fail to read their puppy's signals during play and forget that their puppy will be looking for appropriate "we're playing" signals in return. Problems can occur if your puppy is unsure if you are actually playing or not. Try to remain aware of your movements, your puppy's body language and take regular breaks to give your puppy some freedom of choice and an opportunity to move away if he feels uncomfortable.

Successful game play involves trust between the players.

RIGHT Sometimes the excitement of the game gets all too much — try to learn the signs so this can be avoided

PROBLEMS DURING BRAIN GAMES

Puppies can easily become overaroused while they play and sometimes this can lead to the frustrated owner stopping playing games altogether. During enjoyable play your puppy will become naturally uninhibited. This is part of what makes playing so much fun. Unfortunately, this means that it is easier for him to become overaroused and to do things that he normally wouldn't, such as harder mouthing or jumping up at you.

Mouthing Owners often become concerned about puppy play because of the amount of mouthing that can occur. Your puppy does not have hands with which to move objects around or grab or tickle you; he only has his mouth. Therefore, it is very important to spend time teaching your puppy which objects he is allowed to grab hold of. He has to be taught to be careful when he does use his mouth, and that teeth touching a person's body or clothing will probably end the game.

Mounting Another alarming result of high arousal during play is that some puppies will mount their owner or an item. Puppies of both sexes can do this. Try to stay calm so that you do not create more arousal or draw attention to this action. Quietly stop the game and move away. It is important that you observe your puppy during future games to allow you to notice when he is becoming overexcited. This is not something to worry too much about; some mounting is normal during play and changing hormone levels may make this more likely during adolescence. Mounting can also be an indication that your puppy is finding the interaction stressful and so it may be necessary to rethink the type and style of game play.

LEFT Overarousal can lead to pestering behavior when you don't welcome it.

Lack of progress Don't become frustrated if your puppy is not responding as you expected. Take time out to think about what might be going wrong. Perhaps try a different play style and see if you can find something else that motivates your pup. Usually poor communication is the reason for a lack of desire to play or for the lesson not sticking. Make sure that your reward timings are more accurate, that you are responding appropriately and that your puppy feels confident in the task that you are aiming to do.

LEFT Check your puppy's mouth regularly — new teeth and sore gums can cause pain and so reduce his desire to play games

Lack of interest It is normal for a puppy to be interested in playing. If your puppy suddenly loses his desire to play and interact with you, then it would be sensible to seek advice from your veterinarian. Besides actual illness, there are some common reasons for reduced desire to play which include:

- **New teeth** A teething puppy may become less inclined to play with certain toys for a short period of time while his mouth is at its most sensitive. You may see spots of blood, and occasionally a lost tooth after play. Some other puppies become more frantic when they do play, leading to more intense biting, grabbing and reduced focus. It is important to check your puppy's mouth regularly and to remember that he may be experiencing discomfort.
- **Anxiety** It is easy to appreciate that feeling anxious or frightened will reduce your puppy's wish to play—we humans experience a similar response. If your puppy is new, or has come from a place where he was not exposed to different events and objects, he simply may feel overwhelmed. Take care to interact with him in a way that makes him feel comfortable. Take your time and allow him to familiarize himself with the house and learn to trust you before you begin asking for more. Keep yourself small and avoid sudden big movements.
- **Growing pains** During the growth stages some puppies appear to experience growing pains. They may limp or appear less inclined to join in with activities. Seek advice from your veterinarian.

STOP THE GAME!

It is important to watch your puppy carefully during play so that you can make the right decisions about calming things down, either directing him to another activity or stopping the game entirely.

Stop if you see:

- Your puppy starting to appear stressed or uncomfortable.
- Your puppy's activity levels becoming excessive: lots of leaping, jumping and grabbing.
- Your puppy has switched to mounting or mouthing at you instead of focusing on the game.
- Your puppy is trying to move away from the game.
- Your puppy has stopped play-bowing and appears to be playing "harder."
- Your puppy is beginning to bark much more frequently and in a higher pitch.
- Your puppy is starting to play-growl more than usual.
- Your puppy appears unable to stop the game, even for a brief pause.

He may not want to let go when you tell him to.

ABOVE If a tugging game starts to get a bit too frantic, it is probably time to take a break.

well. Try saying this as you finish each session or stop for a break. This makes it easy for your puppy to understand when it is all right to stop concentrating or to relax.

"That's the end" It is very useful to teach a signal that tells your puppy that the game, training or interaction is over and that he can move away or do something else. A verbal cue such as "All done" or "Off you go" works

Now it's time to relax.

RIGHT If your puppy is struggling to get away, he's had enough.

EQUIPMENT AND BASIC LESSONS

One thing is for sure: there is no shortage of items and bits of equipment on sale targeted at new puppy owners. Before you spend lots of money on just about everything in the store, consider what your personal requirements will be, taking into account your lifestyle and your puppy's breed and character.

FOR YOU

Treat pouch This is a very useful tool since it allows you to keep a selection of treats close at hand while protecting your clothes from the grease and odor associated with dog food. You can then get into the habit of

RIGHT The right gear: practical clothes, comfortable shoes and treat pouch ready to go.

picking up your pouch every time you grab the leash or start a game. Pouches can also hold essential poo bags, whistles, clickers and extra toys for variety.

The right clothing Playing with your puppy will probably involve lots of time spent on the floor, or at least crouching down. Therefore your best work clothes

are not going to be suitable; after all, it is important that you are relaxed and comfortable too. Mouthy puppies often find clothes with long cuffs, tassels or full skirts too tempting to resist, so you might have to adapt your wardrobe temporarily while your puppy is young.

FOR YOUR PUPPY

Collar When you take your puppy out in public, he must wear a collar and ID tag. However, when you first bring him home, you will have to allow him time to become accustomed to wearing it. Easy games can provide a lovely distraction while he gets used to the collar, but more taxing lessons may be difficult if he constantly loses focus in order to fuss at it. Regularly check that the fit is right by ensuring that you can slip two fingers between your puppy's neck and the collar; they grow so quickly that collars can soon become uncomfortably tight.

Brain games props Different items are suggested throughout this book although you must always remember to assess that any item used is safe, of appropriate size and quality and suits your requirement. Discard damaged items and never leave your puppy unsupervised with items that have not been deemed safe for solo puppy play.

Toys As a puppy owner you already probably own many dog toys too. Each will have a purpose, and your puppy's preferences may change over time and as he learns different tasks. Puppies do like chewing and so toys that are easily damaged should be kept for supervised play. Remember that your puppy explores the world with his mouth, and so any item to which he is given access must be safe in this respect.

LEFT Dogs' toys spend a lot of time in their mouths, so make sure that all playthings are safe to chew

Soft toys These are ideal for puppies, but owners often become frustrated when their puppy promptly chews off the eyes, nose or any limbs and proceeds to pull out the stuffing. Although this is an entirely natural canine behavior, it can be expensive and dangerous. Select toys made specifically for dogs and if your puppy likes to gut the toys, opt for the softies that come without any stuffing. If squeakies cause overarousal or unduly worry your puppy, you can silence them by puncturing the internal plastic squeak box with a wide darning needle.

Balls The most critical thing to take into account is size. Dogs choke on small balls and so you must be very careful if you own another larger dog too. Children's bouncy balls are also extremely dangerous as they are small and easily slip down into the windpipe. At no time should your puppy be allowed to play with these.

BELOW When it comes to toys, dog owners have a lot of options. You will soon discover which are your puppy's personal favorites.

LEFT Looks may vary, but clickers all do the same basic job.

Other props Most of the items featured here can easily be obtained cheaply at secondhand stores or they may even be found in your shed or attic. Whatever item you select, examine it carefully to make sure it doesn't pose a risk to your puppy. If it becomes damaged during use, replace it.

CLICKER TRAINING

A clicker is a simple plastic training tool that has an internal metal tongue that "clicks" when pressed. At first, this "click" will mean nothing to your puppy, but when the sound is paired up with the arrival of a treat, you condition your puppy to respond positively when he hears it in the future. He will begin to respond physically and emotionally as if you have already offered the treat reward, but without you needing to be right beside him at that exact second. Being able to reinforce a behavior from a distance gives you a significant advantage when training. "Marking" very

LEFT A clicker lets you mark actions with a sound that your dog learns to recognize.

specific actions is much easier with the clicker technique, although some people prefer to make a "cluck" sound with their tongue or say a specific unique word as a marker instead. As long as your puppy associates your signal as meaning, "Yes! It's worth doing this again," your training will undoubtedly benefit.
A clicker is not essential for training any of the games in this book, but being ready to praise and encourage your puppy, and to join in the fun, definitely is.

PLAY NO-NO'S!

Although it is great to use your imagination when creating brain games for your puppy, please always use caution if you are trying out new ideas.

Avoid sticks and stones Neither make safe playthings and there are so many alternatives, there is no excuse for taking the risk with them. Puppies regularly swallow stones or pieces of wood, become impaled on sharp points, break their teeth or are accidentally hit by thrown items. Do not use them.

Avoid heavy-impact actions Although many of the games described can be adapted as your puppy grows, they deliberately avoid making a puppy leap around or jump since this may pose a problem for some of them.

RIGHT It's tempting to make puppies jump as they play, but take care as such acrobatics can damage growing joints.

quickly. However, to minimize confusion make sure that you use the same words for particular tasks consistently and that the words are simple and easy to distinguish. Your puppy will take time to learn what the words actually mean, so focus on encouraging an action first and then introduce the cue word just as your puppy performs it correctly. After you have repeated this several times, your puppy will start to link the word and the action together. You can then start to say it the moment before he responds to your lure and then, eventually, you can use it as the trigger for an action.

The stress of impact on young joints and still-growing bones can be damaging.

THE BASIC LESSONS

There are some skills that you should try to teach your puppy before you embark on some of the brain games explained in the following chapters. You will cover these if you attend a training class, but in reality you can begin as soon as your puppy arrives home. Starting with good methods early on is preferable to making mistakes that you then have to backtrack on. Approach the basic lessons just as you would a game, since in this way they will be more fun for both you and your puppy.

If your puppy loves retrieving balls, you can start to introduce the cue word "Fetch" while you play this fun game.

Using verbal commands Since humans rely so much on verbal communication, most dog owners use words to signal their wishes to their puppy. Thankfully dogs respond very well to the different sounds we make and can build associations

1 Sit or crouch down and get your puppy's attention. Hold a treat close to your puppy's nose and allow him to sniff it.

At this stage, keep hold of the treat.

Using hand signals Hand signals are extremely useful in dog training so it is worth practicing these. They clarify your commands while allowing you to signal to your puppy without saying a word. Dogs are acutely aware of body language since that is their main method of natural communication, therefore it is perfectly understandable that they can pick up so much from the way we stand, gesture and move our bodies. This is helpful when your puppy is a distance away, where it is noisy or if your puppy has a hearing impairment. It is also very impressive, not to mention satisfying, to get a response without appearing to have asked for it.

LEFT A puppy will quickly learn to grasp a "vocabulary" of various clearly displayed hand signals, if trained to do so. They are very useful when you are working at a distance from the dog.

PUPPY SIT

This lesson is probably the first thing that most dogs ever formally learn. Having said that, many dogs still do not sit reliably when asked to do so. The key to success is lots of practice. Don't assume that your puppy will automatically do it; train him properly and make sure that he is praised and rewarded for getting it right.

Moving On You will find this lesson useful almost every day, no matter what your routine. If your puppy learns to associate

	INTERACTIVE GAME Puppy and Owner
LOCATION	Where your puppy is relaxed
LEVEL OF DIFFICULTY	☆ **Easy brain exercise**
PROPS	Just some treats

2 Very slowly raise the treat upward and back over his head so that his nose rises to follow it. As his head rises, he naturally lowers his bottom.

3 Release the treat as soon as your puppy's bottom touches the floor and praise him. The movement of your hand begins to signal that you want him to "Sit."

TIP

Practice asking your puppy to "Sit" in different places, such as on either side of you, at a distance from you, in varied locations and on different floor surfaces. See how fast you can get him to respond. Prolong the "Sit" by praising and offering another reward when he stays in position. Then allow him to break position by releasing him with your end phrase, such as "Off you go."

4 Practice this routine a few times until your puppy begins to lower his bottom more quickly and reliably when you start to give your signal. Once your puppy is going into the "Sit" position very easily, start to add in your verbal command, "Sit." Initially, say it just as he is getting into position. This will ensure that he links the word and the action. Once he has made a strong association, you can ask him to "Sit" without a hand gesture and expect him to respond quickly.

"Sit" with pleasant results, it can become a great diversion when he is starting to get worried in later situations, perhaps when at the vet's. Performing an action associated with rewards triggers the part of the brain associated with pleasure and inhibits the parts responsible for worry.

TAKE CARE

At no point should you need to push your puppy into position. Be patient and you'll find that your puppy learns the basics very quickly.

RIGHT By rewarding your puppy for getting into the "Sit," he begins to learn that this is a good position to choose, making it more likely that he will "Sit" the next time.

PUPPY DOWN

This is another common lesson that all dogs should be able to follow. Lying down when asked makes your puppy easier to manage in lots of situations, as well as preparing him for many brain games. Without being taught to go "Down," it can be hard for a puppy to learn to enjoy quiet time, or to settle properly, so this command should definitely feature high up in an owner's list of priorities.

4 Move your hand steadily so that he bends to follow it. His back will naturally arch and his front legs start to lower themselves as his muzzle goes down toward the floor.

5 Bending over is a tricky position for your puppy to sustain and so, in order to get at the treat, he should move into a "Down" position. The moment he does so, release the treat and praise him.

	INTERACTIVE GAME Puppy and Owner
LOCATION	A place where your puppy feels safe
LEVEL OF DIFFICULTY	☆ **Easy brain exercise** Teaching "Sit" first helps
PROPS	A soft carpet, rug or bedding and treats

Moving On Once your puppy can lie down on cue, you can begin to encourage him to "Settle" on a mat or on his bed. A moveable cushion or blanket that you can carry and reposition around the home is a very useful accessory since you can then easily encourage the same lesson in different locations. When you see your puppy getting tired or overstimulated, it is a great habit to encourage him to take time out and to settle on his bed. He might rest, or

1 and **2** Crouch down or sit on the floor beside your puppy. Show him a treat and let him stand and sniff it. Lure him into a "Sit" position to begin.

3 Slowly lower the treat from his nose directly downward toward the floor.

6 Repeat a few times every session over several sessions until your puppy can move quickly into the "Down" position when you move your hand. As he moves into position, start to say your "Down" verbal cue.

STANDING UP Begin to practice this while standing up and gradually get your puppy used to you giving a reduced hand signal, so that you have to stoop less and less to get the right response. Continue to praise and reward your puppy for getting it right.

spend time gnawing away at his chew toy; it does not really matter—as long as he is lying down quietly on his designated rest blanket, this is fine.

Practice with distractions around you and in different locations, but remember that your puppy may hesitate to lie down if he is concerned about something nearby.

PUPPY COME!

Life Skill Achieved: I can have freedom.

This is an essential lesson that allows you to grant your puppy some freedom safely while out and about. This is not typically considered a "game" but if you make the lesson fun or feature it as part of a game, your puppy will be more inclined to return to you. Of course, you may practice it more often too if it seems like fun. If you teach your puppy to return reliably to you, your options for playing interesting games will increase significantly.

1 Begin while your puppy is looking at or sniffing something else in the room. It is often helpful to kneel or crouch at first and gradually move on to standing once he is confident.

2 Call him using an excited voice and your chosen cue, "Come!" It will probably help to waggle his toy down at his eye level or open your hand so that he can see the treats.

3 Continue to encourage him as he approaches and offer a reward or the toy when he arrives.

	INTERACTIVE GAME Puppy and Owner
LOCATION	Start this lesson inside your home and then transfer to areas where there are more distractions, such as the yard and then on walks
LEVEL OF DIFFICULTY	**Variable depending upon level of distraction**
PROPS	Treats, toys and a long training leash to ensure safety while this lesson is being taught

4 Gradually build up the distance over which your puppy has to return and the level of distraction from which need to you call him.

GAMES TO IMPROVE PUPPY RECALL RESPONSES

Chase me! Calling your puppy in an excited voice at the same time as turning and running in another direction is a great way to draw his attention to you and to bring him running after you. As he gets close, you can praise him and offer a reward or his toy. If he starts jumping up or grabbing at you, stop running immediately, allow him to calm down and praise him as soon as he does so. Playing this fun and fast-paced game on flat areas of grass is safe and will burn up lots of energy.

Puppy in the middle If you are walking with another person, you can encourage your puppy to run between you by throwing a toy to one another. Get your puppy interested in it by wiggling it and teasing him a little and then tossing it a short distance to your companion. They can do the same thing. Remember to occasionally let your puppy play with the toy and earn rewards or this game will soon become frustrating and no fun at all.

Tag ! In the child's game "Tag" the aim is for one player to catch another and "touch" or "tag" them. This puppy game does not involve chasing after your puppy, but it does involve getting him used to you touching and taking hold of his collar. By associating the act of taking hold of his collar with rewards, you will make it much easier to get hold of him on walks or when something untoward is occurring where being loose may be dangerous. Many dogs learn not to get too close to their owner as that means the end of their freedom. This can be a frustrating and time-consuming habit. This game teaches your puppy that coming close enough to be touched just increases the availability of rewards and so builds positive associations with the act. This can ultimately reduce the chances of him becoming frightened and snapping if he were grabbed during an emergency.

LEFT Two people play "Puppy in the middle" by rolling a ball or toy between them and encouraging the puppy to chase it.

Let him "win" every now and then!

PART TWO

BRING ON THE BRAIN GAMES

Although playing itself is important to the development of a puppy, games can also help you to teach him important lessons that will prove valuable in the future, both in respect of your puppy's responses toward events, and how he is perceived by others. Although the activities involved in each game may have multiple benefits, the key life skill promoted by a particular game is indicated at the beginning of each game entry. A puppy needs to be exposed to a variety of experiences in order for him to reach his best potential with regards to behavior and training, and so

Life Skills

"I have focus and self-control"	These games help your puppy to learn impulse control and to listen for your cue.
"I can be independent"	Your puppy can spend time on self-directed activity and is not totally reliant upon you for entertainment.
"I have great balance and coordination"	These games help your puppy to develop physical accuracy and ability.
"I am relaxed and confident"	Your puppy is exposed to essential experiences via these games that promote habituation and socialization.
"I can listen and watch carefully"	Your puppy learns to pay attention to you during these activities.
"I can express my natural instincts"	These games provide outlets for actions and behaviors that come naturally to your puppy.
"I am relaxed when handled"	These games promote good handling skills and build positive associations with being touched or lifted.
"I am fun to spend time with!"	These games provide stimulation and entertainment for you both, encouraging interaction and bonding.
"I can have freedom"	These games help to improve responses to your call and to incline your puppy to remain close.

everything you do during his first year will have an effect on how he turns out as an adult dog. It feels like a big task and it is, but don't worry—you will have lots of fun along the way.

BRAIN GAMES GUIDELINES

Alongside the instructions for each brain game in this book you will see some additional information in a colored panel that will help you to choose appropriate games for you and your puppy as well as making sure you're prepared with all the correct equipment.

Location? This tells you about the location best suited for the game.

Level of Difficulty To make it a little easier to know which games to try, each is given a star rating on a scale of 1 to 4. 1 Star = Beginner, 4 Star = Advanced. This is a guide only and some puppies are naturally going to pick up some games quicker than others depending on their breed instincts and body design.

Indication is given if learning another game or skill first will be useful.

Props This is an indication of the items that you'll need to play this game.

Interaction Level Another quick indicator about the type of game is the Interaction Key telling you whether the game is suitable for solo play, or is more interactive. The key takes the following form:

= dog plays game alone

= dog plays with his owner

= dog plays game with more than one person

BRAIN GAMES FOR THE HOME

GAMES FOR BABY BRAINS

Very young puppies will enjoy games that involve their natural exploratory behavior.

When not formally teaching your puppy a new task, you can create easy games that allow him to explore different textures and sounds.

PUPPY SENSORY PLAY

Life Skill Achieved: I am relaxed and confident.

The more events that your puppy experiences and associates with fun and pleasure, the better able he will be to cope when he encounters them again later on. Exposure to great variety during the early months will promote brain development so, provided your puppy is never frightened, the only limit is the bounds of your imagination.

ABOVE
Walking on different surfaces can be daunting for puppies that only know tiles or carpeted areas. Allow your puppy to explore an area where you have set out different sensory props. Offer praise and rewards to encourage him.

Try not to soothe your puppy if he startles at something new, as this may reinforce the idea that there is something to be afraid of. Remain nearby so he can look to you to provide him with support and to boost confidence.

	INTERACTIVE GAME Solo game with some supervision	
LOCATION	Where your puppy is relaxed	
LEVEL OF DIFFICULTY	☆ **Easy brain exercise**	
PROPS	Use your imagination: various toys, bath mats, carpet tiles, noisy items, sand, wobbly surfaces, household items, wheeled items, even people in hats, uniforms or costumes	

BOX OF FUN

Life Skill Achieved: I am relaxed and confident.

This game is a fun way to introduce new textures, sounds and basic search activity within the safety of a simple game. Be prepared that this could become messy!

LEFT Boxes have so many uses in puppy play and training that you are only limited by the boundaries of your own imagination and the sizes of the boxes you obtain. Making use of any extra boxes that arrive with deliveries is an excellent way to ensure they are reused before they end up in recycling.

	INTERACTIVE GAME
	Some supervision recommended
LOCATION	In the main area where your puppy plays
LEVEL OF DIFFICULTY	☆ Easy brain exercise
PROPS	A cardboard box or plastic storage box, shredded paper, toys, treats

If you have a particularly large box on hand, you can cut holes in the side so that your puppy can step inside to explore and search for the hidden treats and toys.

RIGHT An easy way to begin is with a basic box with some shredded paper left inside. Be careful that the paper is not printed with toxic ink. Scatter some of your puppy's favorite biscuits into the box and allow him to explore. You might find that you need to place the box on its side when you first begin this game so that it is easy to access. As he grows and becomes confident in his ability, you can set it the right way up so that he has to clamber into it.

LEFT Hidden toys can be used as a lure instead of food treats. It is a great sight when your puppy emerges triumphantly with a trophy.

Moving On Once your puppy has moved on from this and has learned the "Find It" game, you can advance his search by hiding his toys or treats inside the box.

GIFT WRAPPED

Life Skill Achieved: I can express my natural instincts.

This is a messy but fun way to occupy some of your puppy's time, allowing him to explore and perform natural pulling and tearing activity. It can prolong some of the thrill of giving him something new to play with, boosting his pleasure and helping to encourage him to occupy himself.

Everyone loves receiving gifts and most dogs enjoy the novelty of new items too.

	INTERACTIVE GAME Supervision is recommended
LOCATION	Anywhere familiar to your puppy
LEVEL OF DIFFICULTY	☆ Easy brain exercise
PROPS	A toy, cheap paper (ensure any printing on the paper is with nontoxic ink)

1 This game doesn't need to involve brand new toys unless you choose it to. If you rotate your puppy's toys, you can wrap up one he hasn't seen for a while or wrap up a new puppy chewy instead. Most of the fun in this game is in the act of unwrapping and pulling at the paper.

4 and **5** When he rips the paper, you can praise him. The prize is inside so he will quickly learn that unwrapping is the way to get the goodies.

The wrapping paper has done its job.

2 and **3** Wrapping does not require sticky tape. In fact, the fewer things you use for this game, the safer it is. Wrap the toy and crunch the edges of the paper together so they hold.

Encourage your puppy to sniff and play with the gift.

STAY SAFE

Caution should always be taken at any time of year when gifts are around. Many will contain food or plants that are toxic to puppies. Christmas and Easter are particularly dangerous times for dogs.

Rope toys are interactive and fun.

6 Finish by playing with the unwrapped toy. Take care not to leave a puppy who loves this game around your Christmas presents. While most will only open gifts that have enticing smells, others will spend time happily opening everything under the tree!

Moving On This can later lead on to solo games with more complex activity toys to occupy the puppy while you are absent.

chapter 4

FUN IN THE CRATE

Life Skill Achieved: I can be independent.

Spending time within a crate or pen is necessary for many puppies; it may be at home, in the car or while traveling. Others spend some time in a kennel or run. All of these puppies will require extra simulation to prevent boredom and stress from setting in. Make sure that your puppy has lots of freedom with opportunities to play, socialize and exercise every day. This brain game aims to improve your puppy's experience while inside the crate or pen, but it should not be used to excuse excessive crate use.

1 Hang stuffed activity toys on ropes from the top and sides of the crate to encourage your puppy to reach and pull.

2 They can be made more interesting by attaching the toy to a bungee cord. This can be secured to another part of the crate or something solid outside the pen that can act as a stable anchor. When your puppy grabs the toy and pulls, he will be able to enjoy a tuggy game, but when he releases it the toy will bounce back and may release some treats.

STAY SAFE
Never use cords long enough to get wrapped around your puppy's neck or toys that can be easily chewed and broken. This game is best played while you are nearby to supervise it.

	INTERACTIVE GAME Solo game
LOCATION	Wherever your puppy is happy being in his crate
LEVEL OF DIFFICULTY	☆ Easy brain exercise
PROPS	A safe crate free from sharp edges that provides your puppy with enough space to move around. A variety of safe toys and treats

Initially it may help to leave the crate door open. But once your puppy gets absorbed in the game, he will not notice if the door is closed.

3 It can help to feed your puppy while he is in this enclosed area. While scatter feeding here will prolong the activity a little, you might find that your puppy enjoys putting in extra effort to get his food from a variety of activity toys. Select a style and size of toy that suits your puppy. By stuffing food inside these toys, you attract your puppy's attention and encourage him to chew on and toss the toy around. You might need to make the food easy to access at first, but as your puppy becomes more skilled, your stuffing technique will have to adapt to increase the challenge.

4 Force biscuits between the bars of the crate — some low down and others higher up — to keep your puppy sniffing happily and to vary the difficulty of pulling them out.

Moving On As your puppy matures and feels less need to explore everywhere, you should find it easier and safer to leave him with more freedom. He may love having the option of going into his open crate or you may dispense with it entirely.

ACTIVE GAMES

Although your puppy will have to observe some limitations while he grows and his joints become stronger, it is important to encourage some activities and teach games that help him to develop good coordination, spatial awareness and to channel some of that abundant puppy energy in an appropriate way.

SPIN-SPIN

Life Skill Achieved: I am fun to spend time with.

Learning to spin on cue is a simple game that most puppies will pick up after just a few lessons. It is a fun activity that can be enjoyed as a straightforward performance trick but which also leads to some practical benefits, such as asking your puppy to Spin-Spin on a towel or absorbent mat to dry off his feet when coming into the house or before jumping in the car. This is much more entertaining than regular hand toweling.

1 Crouch down in front of your puppy. Hold a treat in one hand and allow your puppy to sniff at it to develop his interest in it.

2 Very slowly, while your puppy sniffs and licks at the treat, move your hand around to the side so that he begins to turn to follow it. Reward him.

3 Release the treat when your puppy succeeds at partial turns rather than expecting a full 360-degree spin in one go. Build up the degree of turn so that your puppy is able to turn confidently in order to follow your hand. Choose your cue word and add it in while your puppy is turning, "Spin."

	INTERACTIVE GAME Puppy and Owner
LOCATION	In an area where your puppy can turn around easily. A nonslippery floor is preferable
LEVEL OF DIFFICULTY	☆ Easy brain exercise
PROPS	Some treats or a favorite toy

4 When your puppy has mastered the first stage you can begin to teach the game while standing up, and then gradually start to minimize the hand gesture. This means that instead of moving your hand in the full circle, you begin to raise it away from your puppy's nose and reduce the size of the movement. If you have practiced enough, your puppy will be able to build on his existing knowledge and respond to a tiny hand signal, or even just the verbal cue by itself.

TIP

It is important that your puppy does not begin to spin in order to gain your attention. Spinning should only be reinforced when it is performed as a response to you giving the cue word.

STAY SAFE

Spinning can be observed in some dogs as a compulsive disorder that disrupts normal behavior. In these cases you should not encourage the spinning game, and instead seek advice from your veterinarian regarding the issue.

5 The movement should be slow and steady with plenty of time allowed between each repetition. As your puppy matures and is physically able to do more, you can increase the number of spins as well as speeding up the game.

Moving On You might also wish to teach your puppy to turn in the opposite direction and give this a new cue word so that he can eventually turn in either direction on cue.

TWIRLING AROUND

Life Skill Achieved: I have great balance and coordination.

This game can be played from a seated position. You will need a stick or an umbrella or some other upright object for your puppy to weave around. Make sure that he is not wary

of this object and is happy to approach it, even when you move it or wobble it around.

Moving On You may wish to expand this game later when your puppy spends more time outdoors. As he matures, he may be able to join an agility class or participate in doggy-dancing, building on these early lessons with ease and confidence.

	INTERACTIVE GAME Puppy and Owner
LOCATION	Where your puppy is relaxed
LEVEL OF DIFFICULTY	☆☆ Moderate brain tester
PROPS	An umbrella, a stick or a pot and treats

THE CHAIR CHA-CHA

Life Skill Achieved: I have great balance and coordination.

To follow on naturally from "Twirling Around," you can teach your puppy to move around the legs of your chair and your feet while you remain seated. You should be able

to comfortably bend over to do this game, or sit on the floor beside the chair if that seems easier.

Moving On This game is perfect for tiny puppies, but as your dog grows it may become more difficult or even impossible for your puppy to continue. Don't worry though since you can either choose to encourage him to crawl through the space as in "Puppy Shuffle" if his size allows, or move on to more traditional weave games such as the one described in "In and Out and Round About" (see page 82).

	INTERACTIVE GAME Puppy and Owner
LOCATION	Any room where your puppy is comfortable
LEVEL OF DIFFICULTY	☆☆ Moderate brain tester
PROPS	A basic, well-balanced chair and your treats

2 Use a food lure to encourage your puppy to move around the umbrella in the right way. As soon as he does, reward him with the treat and praise. As you practice more, you can add in your cue word "Twirl" as he moves around the chosen object.

Over several sessions you should reduce your lure until your puppy can move around the umbrella without so much assistance from you.

1 Hold the umbrella out vertically so that your puppy has space to walk underneath your arm and between it and your chair. If you have trouble holding the umbrella, then try using a free-standing item like a plant pot or even a tall cat-scratching post if you have one in the room.

3 You may need a little practice working out which hand to use and when, but if you place your treat pouch on your lap, you will have both hands free for this game while still having easy access to more rewards when needed.

This weave is turning into a figure-eight.

1 As in the "Twirling Around" game, you should use your treat to lure your puppy under your leg and around the chair leg.

2 As he follows your hand and moves under your leg, be sure to praise and reward each achievement.

51

BRING IT BACK

Life Skill Achieved: I can have freedom.

It is often expected that puppies should automatically bring an item back if you roll or throw it for them. While many puppies will do this wonderfully, it is not something that necessarily works for all. For many it depends upon what the item is and what mood the puppy is in. Creating a fun game where your puppy has a great time retrieving items builds great skills for future activities.

Your eventual aim may be to get the toy returned and perfectly presented to you, as is expected when you take part in competitive sports. However, when first starting, it's best to focus on making this game straightforward fun.

1 Kneel on the floor with your puppy and wiggle the toy to build his interest.

2 Toss or roll it a short distance, making sure not to be too adventurous too soon. Your puppy could easily become distracted if you expect him to run a long distance to get the toy and your enthusiastic encouragement may not have the same impact.

NAME GAME You can play this game with different toys or retrieve items and teach your puppy to distinguish between them by using different names.

Brightly colored toys make great targets for a long-distance retrieve.

Once your puppy has mastered a basic retrieve, try to practice with different toys and with other distractions around. If he can cope with squabbling siblings in the same room, he's doing fine!

	INTERACTIVE GAME Puppy and Owner
LOCATION	Begin in a quiet area of the house and move on to outdoor locations as your puppy gains experience
LEVEL OF DIFFICULTY	☆☆ **Moderate brain tester**
PROPS	Begin with a toy that your puppy really enjoys and can lift and carry without a struggle

3 As your puppy reaches and grabs the toy, call out praise to him and respond in an excited way.

Be aware of your body language so that you do not appear threatening as he approaches. If your puppy is shy at all, avoid direct eye contact, turn slightly away from him and don't reach out toward him as he gets close. Praise and encourage him all the way until he has returned to you.

4 Avoid the temptation to grab the toy right away. Praise and pet your puppy first to make sure that he knows that it was great fun coming back to you. Offer a treat with one hand while you gently cup the toy with the other, waiting for him to let it go.

When he lets the toy go, say "Drop. Good boy" to add in the verbal cue.

1 Over time, you can increase the distance over which your puppy has to practice a retrieve.

2 As an extra reward for bringing it back, end the game by offering a final treat and praise and giving the "end" signal, "All done," while you put the toy away.

Moving On Your puppy may enjoy working on harder retrieves where the item is at a much greater distance before you give the release cue to fetch it, or where he has to sit by you and wait until you give the "Go get it" signal. You can work on teaching the retrieve with many different items and use this game to build up to a really useful search game where your puppy can find your keys or other items that you wish to locate. You can also use this to build a game where he retrieves specific toys after learning their name.

STEP UP

The easiest way to encourage your puppy to "Step Up" is to use a food lure.

Life Skill Achieved: I am fun to spend time with.

1 Allow your puppy to sniff the treat in your hand but don't let him have it. Slowly raise the treat from his nose to a position above the step.

	INTERACTIVE GAME Puppy and Owner
LOCATION	Any room where your puppy is comfortable
LEVEL OF DIFFICULTY	☆ Easy brain exercise
PROPS	A strong box or a small step, treats

This is a great cue to get your puppy to pose for a picture or for a puppy to raise himself up a little to allow an owner with back problems to clip on the leash more easily. This is good for larger dogs that you do not want to jump up on a chair for handling.

BURIED TREASURE

Life Skill Achieved: I can express my natural instincts.

This is an exciting and easy search game that can provide a useful outlet for puppies that love to dig and burrow.

1 Let your puppy watch while you tuck his toy under the edge of the blanket.

	INTERACTIVE GAME Puppy and Owner
LOCATION	Inside
LEVEL OF DIFFICULTY	☆☆ Moderate brain tester
PROPS	A favorite toy, a blanket or duvet

Moving On You may wish to encourage your puppy to dig in a sandpit to search for buried toys and treats. Directing your puppy's digging instincts in this way is preferable to him damaging your yard.

2 In order to follow the treat he will have to step up with his front feet. When he does, immediately release the treat and praise him.

Keep practicing until he can easily place both paws up on the step. You can then add in your verbal cue, "Step Up."

3 Eventually you will be able to ask him to "Step Up" without the lure.

2 Encourage him to "Find" the toy. Praise him for making efforts to get the toy by digging and rummaging around.

If your puppy cannot manage to uncover the toy from underneath a blanket, you can make this game simpler by hiding the toy underneath a pile of cushions, or tucked underneath his soft puppy bedding.

3 When he finds the toy, praise him and join him for a quick game.

STAY SAFE

It is never appropriate for children to hide under the blanket as a target for the puppy to jump on, or seek out. There is a risk of mouthing or scratching occurring.

4 Next time you play, tuck the toy slightly further under the blanket, making it a little bit harder to get to. Eventually the toy will be entirely concealed underneath and your puppy will have to spend more time and energy working out ways to uncover it.

TUGGY-TUGGY

Life Skill Achieved: I have focus and self-control.

While still an activity that causes some owners alarm, teaching a controlled tug game can instill a great level of self-control while providing a stimulating and exciting activity. This game should not teach aggression or encourage competitive behavior as long as you are careful in the way you respond. It is not necessary to "win" every game (since doing so will make this rather tedious for your puppy), but do ensure that you initiate the game and end when you feel he has had enough.

Keeping in control

If your puppy is so excited that he continues anyway, then end the game by saying something like "Enough" while dropping the toy abruptly and turning and walking away. By removing yourself from the game it

1 Select a toy large enough for your puppy to grab, while your hand holding the other end remains a safe distance away.

This is an exciting game and initially your puppy might get too enthusiastic and grab at the wrong place. A soft toy or rope toy are ideal options since they are soft enough to be comfortable in your puppy's mouth. Other rubber options are available and your puppy's preferences may vary as he grows. This toy should only be your "tuggy" toy. Do not leave it out for your puppy to play with at other times. Do not participate in tuggy-tuggy games with other toys.

becomes less exciting for your puppy and he will begin to learn about the consequences of not listening to you.

In the event that your puppy manages to pull the toy from your hand, resist chasing after him. Sit quietly and wait for him to come back to you once he realizes the tuggy game doesn't work by himself.

It is best to manage the game so that only appropriate behavior is learned. Do not worry if your puppy tends to respond in one of the above ways as long as you work to teach better control. This impulse control is very important later in life.

	INTERACTIVE GAME Puppy and Owner
LOCATION	In a place where your puppy feels safe and with enough room to move around
LEVEL OF DIFFICULTY	☆☆ **Moderate brain tester**
PROPS	A toy selected to be used as a tug-toy now and in the future, and treats. A second tug-toy may be useful

2 Get down close to the floor (although if your puppy is particularly boisterous or mouthy then please try to sit up to keep your face out of reach—an excited puppy can sometimes make a mistake).

3 Wiggle the toy at floor level in front of your puppy. You may find that letting him approach and sniff it before you start wiggling it will increase his interest and encourage him to mouth at it.

4 When your puppy is holding on to the toy, praise him and say "Tuggy-Tuggy!" to show him what game you are playing. Later, when you give this signal, he will know what game you want him to play.

STAY SAFE

This game is never suitable for young children since they are unlikely to maintain sufficient control. They often perform tug games with a variety of toys or clothing and while running around. This creates a high-risk situation for unwanted behavior and is best avoided.

5 Encourage your puppy to release the toy by praising him when he does so, "Drop, good boy!" If your puppy lets go of the tug-toy, then you can invite him to play again, wiggling it and saying "Tuggy-Tuggy."

TROUBLESHOOTING

Not all puppies have great self-control at first. If he needs help in letting go, do not pull at the toy or pry his mouth open. Instead just stop pulling the toy and wait quietly for him to pause to assess the situation.

If your puppy is one that stops tugging but still keeps hold of the tug-toy, then you can encourage him to let go by offering him a treat from your free hand, or by wiggling a second tug-toy (kept in your pocket or tucked into your waistband for easy access).

Watch your puppy carefully and stop the game before he gets too excited. Some puppies, such as terrier breeds, love this game so much that they find it hard to contain their excitement and this can lead to leaping and mouthing if you let the game go on too long.

YOGA DOG

Life Skill Achieved: I have great balance and coordination.

Many of us have unused yoga balls in the cupboard. These are large inflatable plastic balls that are used to help people perform certain yoga postures and gym exercises. Your puppy could also have lots of fun with

![silhouette]	INTERACTIVE GAME Puppy and Owner
LOCATION	Any room with a little space to move around
LEVEL OF DIFFICULTY	☆☆☆ **Good brain workout** Your puppy might find it easier if he already knows how to "Step Up"
PROPS	An inflated yoga ball, an air pump

one, so bring it out today and begin your own version of puppy yoga. Your puppy will be mentally stimulated by learning a new activity, and he will also have fun stretching and learning to coordinate his movements with the ball.

1 Using a treat, lure your puppy to step up against the ball. Initially your puppy will just use the ball to lean against in order to get at the treat.

4 Very gradually, working always at your puppy's speed and comfort level, encourage him to walk with the yoga ball as it moves. Depending upon your puppy's physique and personality, he may take to this right away or need lots of encouragement.

5 As your puppy pushes on the ball, you can introduce your chosen verbal cue. Eventually this should be the trigger for your puppy to start the game without further encouragement.

Position the yoga ball so that it cannot roll away. This may mean leaning it up against furniture or stabilizing it yourself. Allow your puppy to explore until he is comfortable and confident.

3 Once he has reached this stage you can begin to encourage a little movement. Position yourself so that you can control the movement of the ball with one hand, or rest it against your body while you lure your puppy up against the ball. Allow the ball to move slightly so that your puppy has to take steps with his back feet to maintain contact with the ball and to reach the treat.

2 Offer the treat as soon as he has placed his paw on the ball. Practice until he is comfortable placing his paws on the ball while he eats the treats you offer.

Moving On Your puppy may get to a stage of being happy to climb onto the yoga ball and balance on top of it. Again this is easier initially if the ball has a little air removed first so that it is soft and easier to balance on. Young puppies should not be encouraged to jump down from the ball as it might damage growing joints. With practice, your puppy may grow to like this game so much that he can balance on top!

TIP

It can be helpful to let out a little air from your ball before you start so that it is easier for your puppy to position his paws on the ball without it moving around so easily. As he improves and grows, you can inflate the ball with more air to help it to roll along more smoothly across the floor.

It is easier for little paws if the ball is slightly deflated to begin with.

In between training sessions you should put the ball away or be prepared to reward your puppy for trying out the game on his own initiative. However, this does pose the risk that it may move too fast or bump into something it shouldn't, so take care.

59

PULL IT!

Life Skill Achieved: I can express my natural instincts.

It can sometimes help if your dog can pull open a door, a cupboard or a drawer for you. Some owners teach this purely for fun, while others find it an important aid to their daily lives. Whatever your reasons, you should think carefully about what you would like your puppy to be able to open as it goes without saying that it is vital that he cannot access anything that could be dangerous.

Moving On When this game has been successfully completed, you could link it with "Where's Your Leash?" (see page 68) if you would prefer to keep the leash tidied away in a drawer. Then your puppy can run to the drawer, open it and collect his leash.

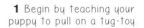

1 Begin by teaching your puppy to pull on a tug-toy.

2 When he can do this well, you can secure one end to a drawer or door handle. Initially you will probably have to hold the tuggy and entice him to take hold of it. When he does, say "Tuggy-Tuggy!" to encourage him to pull on the toy. Praise and reward him for doing so.

	INTERACTIVE GAME Puppy and Owner
LOCATION	In your home by a drawer or cupboard you would like your puppy to open
LEVEL OF DIFFICULTY	☆☆☆☆ **Advanced brain game** Teach your puppy to play "Tuggy-Tuggy" with a rope toy first, then "Where's Your Leash?"
PROPS	A basic, well-balanced cupboard unit and your treats

▬▬ TIP ▬▬

Make sure the tug-toy is long enough to ensure that the door can be pulled open without banging straight into your puppy's face. If that happens, he may never want to play again, so make sure the equipment is correctly positioned from the start. The cupboard may become accidentally scratched while your dog is learning this game, so it is a good idea to protect any vulnerable parts of the surface with some temporary plastic sheeting.

A good tug on the toy will see the door swing open on cue!

3 When the drawer or door opens, praise him and offer him a really great reward! This should keep him enthusiastic despite the unexpected opening of the drawer or door. An empty drawer is easier to start with, so there is no extra weight to pull against.

Keep practicing until he can pull the drawer or door open easily.

4 Add in your new cue word just before the old one so that he begins to make the new association. Say, "Pull, Tuggy-Tuggy" and then praise and reward him for getting the drawer or door open. Practice this over many short training sessions until he begins to tug when he hears the cue "Pull."

5 While you are not training this game, you should unclip the tug-toy from the handle. This is also useful for day-to-day life when you don't want him accessing the cupboard or drawer on his own.

STAY SAFE!

Drawers should have safety stops to prevent them from being pulled out completely. Some dogs will use an open drawer as a "step-up" onto countertops. Consider these factors and then decide whether you would like to teach this game to your puppy.

Although your puppy would love it, it is best not to practice this with the drawer or cupboard in which his treats are stored away!

INTO MY ARMS

Life Skill Achieved: I am relaxed and easy to handle.

Teaching your puppy to jump up into your arms on cue can be useful since it allows your puppy to play an active role in this embrace, rather than suddenly being scooped up unexpectedly. Clearly this is a game that in practical terms can only be taught to tiny breeds of dog since the implications of trying this with a fully grown Labrador or Leonberger are not pleasant to contemplate! This is a helpful skill if you struggle to bend all the way down to lift up your puppy.

	INTERACTIVE GAME Puppy and Owner
LOCATION	Any room where your puppy is comfortable and with space to get a little speed up on approach
LEVEL OF DIFFICULTY	☆☆ Moderate brain tester
PROPS	Treats, cushions and a low chair

This game should not encourage a puppy to jump up as a way of gaining your attention provided you only reward him after you have first given the cue signal. In fact, once an action is put "on cue" like this, it becomes much easier to manage at other times.

1 Crouch or kneel down and call your puppy to you excitedly, tapping your thighs with your hands.

4 Gradually raise yourself into a higher position. Depending upon the size and age of your puppy, you might want to sit on cushions or on a low chair.

5 Repeat this stage until your puppy is very comfortable with running up and into your arms when you give the signal.

2 If your puppy is very excited to run toward you, you are off to a flying start with this game as the aim is for him to jump onto your lap, or at least place his front feet up to start with.

3 As he hops onto your lap, continue to praise him while you gently place your hands on him as if you're holding him. Offer a treat while he is in your arms. Then gently put him back on the floor.

As you practice, start to say your cue word, "Up" or "My Arms" as he hops onto your lap.

STAY SAFE! Never allow your puppy to leap from your arms to the ground from a height. This jarring impact could potentially cause injury to young joints and still-growing bones.

Later begin to stand up straight. Initially you might need to lean against the wall with your legs slightly bent, so that your puppy can use your thighs as a platform. When attempting this while free-standing, have one knee bent to make the game easier for your puppy

RAISING THE BAR Over time, raise yourself onto a chair and teach your puppy to jump up confidently onto your lap. Remember to continue to praise and reward him for jumping up on cue.

SEARCH GAMES
FOOD FORAGE

Life Skill Achieved: I can be independent.

This is a very easily organized game that will take advantage of your puppy's natural foraging instincts without you having to spend a lot of time teaching him a new game. This is a great game to play if you want to prolong the time that your puppy takes to eat his food, or to create a valuable distraction while you hang out the laundry or even catch a couple of minutes of relaxation time while you can.

	INTERACTIVE GAME Solo game
LOCATION	In your yard
LEVEL OF DIFFICULTY	☆ Easy brain exercise
PROPS	A bowl of dry puppy food

The foraging instinct can be utilized without needing to use up your puppy's entire meal. A few scattered treats will work well for a shorter period of distraction and can be a great alternative behavior to redirect the attention of a puppy who wants to consume his feces immediately after pooping.

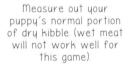

Measure out your puppy's normal portion of dry kibble (wet meat will not work well for this game).

1 Take the bowl into your yard. Keep hold of the bowl while you fling the kibble contents all over the ground so they spread out. This area must be free from dog feces, fragile plants, yard chemicals and anything else that you would not want your puppy to encounter.

2 Your puppy will have to search for each piece. Scatter-feeding like this can also be useful indoors if the food and flooring are suitable for the purpose.

Occupying him like this while you pick up the feces can help to create desirable new habits in a stress-free way.

Puppies generally love these toys—treats while you play, what could be better?

This food-dispensing toy is shaped like a ball with small holes through which food can scatter.

3 Alternative foraging games can be played by placing dry puppy food and treats inside a toy food dispenser. These come in different styles which the puppy can push or roll about so that they drop biscuits through small apertures as they move. Plastic drink bottles can also be used as fun dispensers although care should be taken to discard them once they become cracked or chewed. These types of food-dispensing toys can be used indoors and out and may be a more suitable option than scattering food on the ground in some situations.

STAY SAFE

Don't scatter food around delicate plants or cocoa mulch (the material left over from the cocoa bean roasting process that is used as mulch) as your puppy is likely to cause damage to the plants or ingest the mulch, which can be toxic to dogs.

FIND IT

Life Skill Achieved: I can express my natural instincts.

Learning to focus on finding hidden items is an excellent way to utilize your puppy's time and energy. You can start indoors while your puppy is small, leading on to games in the yard and then while on walks too. All breeds will enjoy this activity at some level if you find something to hide that really motivates

1 While your puppy is gently held by a helper, you should tease him with a favorite toy before tucking it just out of sight behind furniture or a cushion. At this stage it should be very easily and quickly accessed by your puppy.

your puppy. Keeping his brain focused on the hidden item can help to distract him from other unwanted activities.

Moving On This game can be kept simple, or advance into search games covering large areas or searching for specific items.

	**INTERACTIVE GAME** Puppy, Owner and helper
LOCATION	Begin in a room familiar to your puppy and then move on to new areas as skills improve
LEVEL OF DIFFICULTY	☆☆☆ **Good brain workout**
PROPS	Dry puppy biscuits, biscuit jar or box (for game below), a toy

WHERE'S THE BISCUIT?

Life Skill Achieved: I am fun to spend time with.

Your puppy will quickly learn where you keep the dog biscuits. However, it's fun to teach him to respond by running to the biscuit box when you say, "Where's the Biscuit?" This is fairly easy to teach since the association is so quickly made between the location and the treats.

1 Pick a quiet time to begin training or do this when you are going to offer a dog biscuit anyway.

In an excited voice say to your dog, "Biscuits!" Then rush to the biscuit jar or cupboard where they are kept. You puppy will probably rush there along with you.

2 Without delay tell your puppy to "Find It," while your helper releases him. Encourage him to the right location and praise him for finding it. Depending on his preferences you may need to play with your puppy and his toy, or allow him to run around on his own with his prize before trying the game again.

3 As you practice, you should be able to move the toy a little further out of sight, or delay the moment slightly before you release your puppy to "Find It." Resist the temptation to push on too fast before you are sure that your puppy understands the game at the level you are working on.

HIDDEN TREAT One way to expand this game in a confined space is to hide the treat under a pot or cup and encourage your puppy to search for the treat. Start with a single pot and hide the treat while your puppy watches.

Once your puppy is confident with this starting point, you can add in extra pots and add further complexity by moving them about before you ask him to find the treat.

2 Take a treat out and reward him. Repeat this until he anticipates your response and starts toward the location of the biscuits himself when he hears you say the cue "Biscuits!"

3 Over time, practice from farther away from the cupboard or jar and then try the game while other distractions are happening around you and the puppy.

Moving On This can be an excellent distraction as you anticipate the mail arriving or someone coming to the door. By teaching your puppy to respond by going to the biscuit jar instead of rushing to the door, you build a great routine that minimizes troublesome issues like barking at the mail carrier or jumping up at visitors.

WHERE'S YOUR LEASH?

Life Skill Achieved: I am fun to spend time with.

This game teaches your puppy to fetch his own leash in preparation for your walks together. Most dogs view going on a walk as one of the best parts of their day and so they are usually happy to learn any game associated with this time of eager anticipation.

	INTERACTIVE GAME **Puppy and Owner**
LOCATION	In your house with access to the dog leash
LEVEL OF DIFFICULTY	☆☆☆ **Good brain workout** Teach a "Bring It Back" command first
PROPS	Your dog's leash and some treats

Moving On If your puppy reaches an advanced level of training, you could keep the leash in a drawer or cupboard and teach him to open it, as in "Pull It!," and get the leash out. This is an extra-challenging brain game.

━━━ TIP ━━━

While you are training your dog to do this game, you should keep the leash out of sight between training sessions. If not, you must be prepared to praise and reward your puppy if he picks up the leash at other times when you have not asked for it.

1 Start in a part of the house that is near where the leash is kept. Encourage your puppy to take hold of his leash by holding it out to him and telling him to "Take it."

4 Ask a member of your family to gently hold your puppy at a short distance while you place the leash on the floor near to where it will be kept. They can then release him when you encourage him to fetch it.

Wait until he has come forward and picked up the leash and then praise him and reward again. He now understands that picking up the leash will bring him rewards.

Encourage him as he brings the leash to you.

Once he is doing this reliably you can add in your cue word "Leash" (as in "Fetch Your Leash").

2 When he takes it in his mouth, praise him, and then gently take the leash from him while offering a reward. Never engage in a tuggy game with the leash.

Increase the time that your puppy holds onto the leash by pausing before you take the leash from him.

3 Play a game of fetch with the leash so that your puppy starts to learn to pick it up and return it to you. Some puppies find it simpler if the leash is folded and tied so that it is easy to pick up.

5 If you play this when you are ready to go on a walk, then his reward will be very exciting and satisfying as you will clip the leash on and take him right out. This is sure to increase his enthusiasm for this game.

6 When you reach the final stages of the game, he will start to realize that he will not receive his rewards unless you have specifically asked him for his leash. Of course, there is still a distinct possibility that he will begin to go and get it of his own accord when he anticipates that it is time for his walk!

Ask him to "Sit" while you clip on the leash.

PARTY GAMES
HOW MANY PUPPY PAWS?

Life Skill Achieved: I am relaxed when handled.

In this game your puppy learns to lift each foot in turn. Giving labels to the individual feet or numbering the paws is a fun game, but it has practical uses too since it creates a predictable game that can help your puppy to relax while you are drying his feet or checking his paws for seeds, thorns or mud trapped between the pads. Linking this physical contact with the arrival of rewards will create positive emotions, reducing the likelihood of your puppy wanting to avoid having his feet handled.

1 Begin with your puppy in a standing position. Start with just one leg initially to reduce any potential confusion. Gently touch the back of the leg to encourage him to lift that paw. When he does, praise him and offer a reward.

CHECKING PADS Once your puppy has become accustomed to having his feet handled, you will be able to check his pads for cracks or thorns without undue fuss.

	INTERACTIVE GAME Puppy and Owner
LOCATION	In your home with few distractions
LEVEL OF DIFFICULTY	☆ Easy brain exercise
PROPS	Treats

2 When you have succeeded with one foot, you should move on to another and repeat the task until he understands this development of the game. Reward him as he progresses.

3 Don't try asking for different feet to be presented during the same session until he has a really good grasp of each individual cue.

Repeat a few times. Your puppy should begin to lift the leg more quickly as you practice this action.

When he will happily lift the leg, you can label it with a number or a name. It is easy to number the feet Paw One, Paw Two and so forth, but you must remember which foot is which when you play the game again!

EARS AND TEETH When he is comfortable with you stroking and lifting his legs and feet, he will be much more inclined to sit quietly while you proceed to check ears and teeth.

Moving On When your puppy is quite happy having each foot held, you can begin gradually to build up the length of time for which you hold it and the amount of stroking that you perform. Begin to practice this game while out and about, so that he is completely comfortable should you need to check his paw to remove a thorn during a walk.

TAKE A BOW

Life Skill Achieved: I am fun to spend time with.

1 Bend down with your puppy standing in front of you. Hold a treat in front of his nose but don't let him eat it yet.

	INTERACTIVE GAME Puppy and Owner
LOCATION	Wherever your puppy is relaxed enough to concentrate
LEVEL OF DIFFICULTY	☆☆ **Moderate brain tester** Teach your puppy a reliable "Down" command first to avoid confusion
PROPS	Treats

Bowing down is a play gesture that naturally occurs in dogs. Your puppy will spontaneously perform this action himself, but he can also be taught to bow on cue which makes a lovely act to tag on to the end of your trick performances!

TELL ME A SECRET!

Life Skill Achieved: I am fun to spend time with.

In this game your puppy appears to whisper in your ear when you ask him to tell you a secret. Luckily the secret of this game is that it is easy to teach as long as your puppy is relaxed and if you don't mind a little doggy breath in your ear! With

practice, most puppies will learn to do this fairly quickly, though the final challenge is to get him to confess to you what he's really thinking about!

1 Begin sitting on the floor or in a position where your puppy can easily reach your ear.

	INTERACTIVE GAME Puppy and Owner
LOCATION	Any room where your puppy is comfortable
LEVEL OF DIFFICULTY	☆☆ **Moderate brain tester**
PROPS	Treats

2 Slowly lower your hand from his nose downward toward the floor.

As soon as your puppy dips his head down to follow, praise him and let him eat the treat. Repeat and practice until your puppy can dip his head further down before you offer the reward. Timing is important since if you delay releasing the reward, your puppy will move into a full "Down" position.

Gradually begin to prolong the time your puppy bows before you praise and reward him.

3 When your puppy can bend down into a bow, you can add in your verbal cue "Bow." Reward him for correct responses. Begin to give the cue "Bow" and the gesture but without holding a treat in your hand. Instead, when he moves into a bow offer him a reward from the other hand.

3 Repeat this stage until he automatically sniffs at your ear when you point at it, even when you are not holding a treat. Reward from the other hand instead. When he has learned to do this, you can add in your cue word, "Secret." Now, every time he goes to sniff at your ear when you point, you should say "Secret" and offer a reward for getting it right.

2 Teach this by holding a treat between finger and thumb by your earlobe as a lure to encourage a sniff. Some people prefer to rub a treat on their earlobe but this should not be necessary. Never put a treat inside your ear as it could damage your ear canal. Encourage your puppy to sniff your hand; when he does, praise him and offer him the reward.

STAY SAFE

Do not teach this game with excitable puppies or those going through a difficult play-biting stage. Those puppies should never have the chance to make contact with your face, since mistakes are easily made and you may get a nip as a consequence.

SHAKE A PAW

Life Skill Achieved: I am relaxed when handled.

Many puppy owners begin with this trick as puppies will naturally use their feet to touch and paw during play and interaction. Although some people rely on grabbing the paw, it is very easy to teach your puppy to offer his feet on cue.

1 Sit on the floor in front of your puppy. Hold a treat in one hand and close your fist around it.

INTERACTIVE GAME	
Puppy and Owner	
LOCATION	In a quiet area of your home
LEVEL OF DIFFICULTY	☆ Easy brain exercise
PROPS	Treats

▨▨▨▨ TIP ▨▨▨▨

Some puppies will paw at their owner when they want attention. Many people find this unacceptable behavior so make sure that when he does this inappropriately, you ignore him and avoid giving him any attention. Of course, do think about what he might need, since this may be a way of asking to go outside. Wait for a moment and then act once he has stopped pawing at you.

CHANGE PAWS Puppies tend to be either left- or right-pawed! So once you have taught this command with his first choice, try it with the other paw too. Usually this involves holding the treat in a different position so that you encourage your puppy to bear weight on the other foot.

Puppies vary in their responses: holding the treat closer to the unused paw often encourages them to use that one, while others can be tempted if you hold it toward the opposite side. Explore what works with your puppy. Remember to use a different cue word when shaking this other paw.

2 Hold this hand in front of your puppy at chest height so that he can sniff, but not access, the treat. Wait quietly and patiently while he investigates your hand and decides how he can get to the food. If your puppy tries mouthing your hand, avoid yelling or jerking it away as this will increase the likelihood of more mouthing. Try to ignore these attempts and wait so that they are unsuccessful. If your puppy mouths too hard for comfort, quietly withdraw and try again later.

Practice until he is more confident at raising that paw and will raise it onto your hand.

3 After a short delay, most puppies will lift a paw in an attempt to get at the treat. As soon as this happens, open your hand and let him eat the food. It doesn't matter if your puppy only raises his paw very slightly, any movement should be reinforced to make it clear that it is what you want from him.

Moving On Once your puppy knows this command, you can start to introduce useful new experiences such as checking his paws, drying them with a towel and even clipping his nails. Each of these must be introduced very slowly; take your time and break them down into small, achievable stages. Make sure your puppy feels relaxed and rewarded throughout.

4 Add in your verbal cue "Shake" as he performs the movement. Once this is paired up with the action, you can say it when you want him to play the game.

CROSS YOUR LEGS

Life Skill Achieved: I am fun to spend time with.

This game involves teaching your puppy to cross one front leg over the other while he's lying down. It works best with longer legs so the game may need to wait until your puppy has grown or you must adapt it for short-legged dogs.

Use a treat to gain your puppy's attention.

	INTERACTIVE GAME Puppy and Owner
LOCATION	Where your puppy can lie down comfortably
LEVEL OF DIFFICULTY	☆☆☆ **Good brain workout** Teach your puppy to go "Down" and to readily "Shake a Paw" first
PROPS	Treats

1 Ask your puppy to lie "Down" in front of you. Ask him to "Shake" so that he starts to lift one paw from this "Down" position. Praise and reward him.

Practice this stage several times to get him accustomed to performing while in the "Down." Ideally your puppy will now offer his paw when you extend your hand as he can predict what you want from him. If this occurs, you can start to drop out the "Shake" cue in preparation for your new one later.

Moving On Since puppies usually prefer to use one paw rather than the other, begin with the paw he is most eager to use.

This time it's left paw going over the right.

Once you've achieved this, attempt the game with the alternative paw, perhaps calling it "Fold Your Arms" to distinguish between the two.

2 Once you are happy that he can do this reliably, you should very gradually start moving your extended hand across toward the left paw. Do this gradually, making sure that your puppy is still confident with each stage. Start practicing the move while holding your hand resting on the left leg.

3 Progress to moving your hand to the side, and just out of reach so that your puppy touches his own leg rather than your hand. Reward him well for this and focus on getting your timing accurate.

4 Once he is doing the move reliably, you should introduce your cue phrase, "Cross Your Legs." Keep practicing until your puppy understands your meaning.

As your puppy gets better at this game, increase the time that he has to hold the position before you offer the reward.

ROLY-POLY PUP

Life Skill Achieved: I am fun to spend time with.

This is a fun trick that puppies of most shapes and sizes can accomplish fairly quickly. You will teach your puppy to follow a cue and roll right over on his back until he is lying on his other side.

1 Sit on the floor with your puppy lying down in front of you. Hold the treat close to his nose.

2 Very slowly move the treat around to the side so that he turns his head to follow it. You will see him shift his weight to make it easy to follow. Offer the treats to encourage each correct movement.

	INTERACTIVE GAME Puppy and Owner
LOCATION	A quiet room where your puppy is comfortable lying down
LEVEL OF DIFFICULTY	☆☆ **Moderate brain tester** Teach your puppy to go "Down" first
PROPS	Treats, a soft flooring

CAN I SEE YOUR BELLY?

Life Skill Achieved: I am relaxed when handled.

This is an easy game for those puppies that have already learned to roll over and have their belly scratched for pleasure. And that probably includes most dogs!

	INTERACTIVE GAME Puppy and Owner
LOCATION	Any location where your puppy is happy to "Roll Over"
LEVEL OF DIFFICULTY	☆☆ **Moderate brain tester** Teach a "Down" and "Roly-Poly Pup" first
PROPS	Treats and a mat if the flooring is hard or cold

TIP

If your puppy seeks petting by approaching confidently and rolling over for a belly rub, you can take advantage of this by giving the action a cue word "Belly." Praise him and give him a rub since that's probably what he really wants most at that moment.

3 Repeat this action until you find your puppy shifting his weight more quickly and starting to roll onto his shoulder and side. This puppy likes a chest scratch as a reward.

4 Once he is rolling over well, you can start to introduce your verbal cue "Roll Over." To reduce reliance on the food lure, begin to offer the reward from your other hand instead of the one used for the lure/gesture.

Gradually begin to practice while crouching down and then standing so that your puppy becomes accustomed to responding while you are in a more natural training position.

With practice, your puppy should roll over when he sees your signal and hears your verbal cue.

Continue the movement by moving the hand with the treat over his body to the other side. As he tries to follow your hand, he will roll over. This is easiest if you make sure that you arc your arm so that there is plenty of space for his legs to move unimpeded as he rolls.

2 Keep practicing this until your puppy rolls onto his back to expose his belly at which point introduce your command cue, "Belly." Say this each time he is starting to roll onto his back. He should begin to link the word with the action.

Once your puppy understands the action, you will be able to fade out the hand signal. Gradually make this smaller until it is simply a slight gesture.

1 Begin with your puppy in a "Down" position in front of you as for "Roly-Poly Pup." Follow the same procedure, but release the treat the moment your puppy has rolled onto his back lying belly up. You will have to be quick in order to reward him before he flops over onto the other side.

79

PUPPY SHUFFLE!

Life Skill Achieved: I have great balance and coordination.

Puppies look cute while crawling and this game can be combined with others in this book to create more challenging obstacle

courses. The shuffle will appear different depending upon your puppy's physique as some comfortably crawl while others prefer to "bunny hop" along. The slow, forward movement involved in this game encourages your puppy to be aware of his limbs in a way that running and bouncing around do not.

	INTERACTIVE GAME Puppy and Owner
LOCATION	On a floor where your puppy is comfortable to lie
LEVEL OF DIFFICULTY	☆☆ **Moderate brain tester** It helps to have taught your puppy to go "Down" first
PROPS	Treats

WHO'S BEHIND YOU?

Life Skill Achieved: I am fun to spend time with.

This simple game will entertain your guests. When you ask your dog "Who's behind you?" he will look around to check behind him.

	INTERACTIVE GAME Puppy and Owner
LOCATION	A place where there are few distractions
LEVEL OF DIFFICULTY	☆☆ **Moderate brain tester**
PROPS	Treats

1 Start with your puppy standing in front of you. Hold a treat out and allow him to sniff at it.

Slowly move the treat toward one of your puppy's shoulders so that he turns his head to follow it. As his head turns, release the treat quickly or he will begin to turn his whole body.

1 Begin with your puppy in a "Down." Hold a treat to his nose and very slowly move it away from him keeping it low to the ground. As soon as he starts to shuffle forward, release the treat and praise him. Don't raise the treat too high or your puppy will get up rather than crawl forward.

2 Repeat this stage, rewarding each forward movement. Keep it simple, rewarding frequently until he can crawl a short distance.

While your puppy is moving forward introduce your verbal cue "Crawl" and reward him.

2 Practice until he can turn quickly and easily. Remember to reward him for getting the move right.

Add in your cue word "Behind" just as he begins to turn his head each time.

3 Once he has made the association with the word, you can begin to fade out the lure so that you are just pointing to his shoulder instead of doing the full hand movement.

With practice you will be able to simply point and say "Who's behind you?" and he will look on cue.

BRAIN GAMES FOR THE YARD
IN AND OUT AND ROUND ABOUT

Life Skill Achieved: I have great balance and coordination.

Most of us with yard areas have spare plant pots, or even some potted plants that we can move around easily. These can become great activity items for your puppy, and may be used in several ways. Allow your puppy to familiarize himself with these and any other prop before you begin the game.

INTERACTIVE GAME	
	Puppy and Owner
LOCATION	In your yard or a large room
LEVEL OF DIFFICULTY	☆ **Easy brain exercise**
PROPS	Four to eight plant pots or exercise cones, treats

1 Position your cones (or plant pots) so that they are well and equally spaced out. Your puppy should be able to walk in between them easily.

Colored cones are light and easy to position to make the obstacle course.

Use a treat to lure your puppy to follow the direction of your hand.

Moving On This game can be performed around any series of posts, and if you plan on attending agility with your puppy, he will almost certainly be expected to try weaving around poles as they form part of a standard agility course (left). The aim is that the faster he is the better, but precision is the key factor; he can't skip any or he will lose points. On walks you might want to improvise and encourage your puppy to weave through open fence posts, or even around trees. Use your imagination to enrich your outdoor experiences.

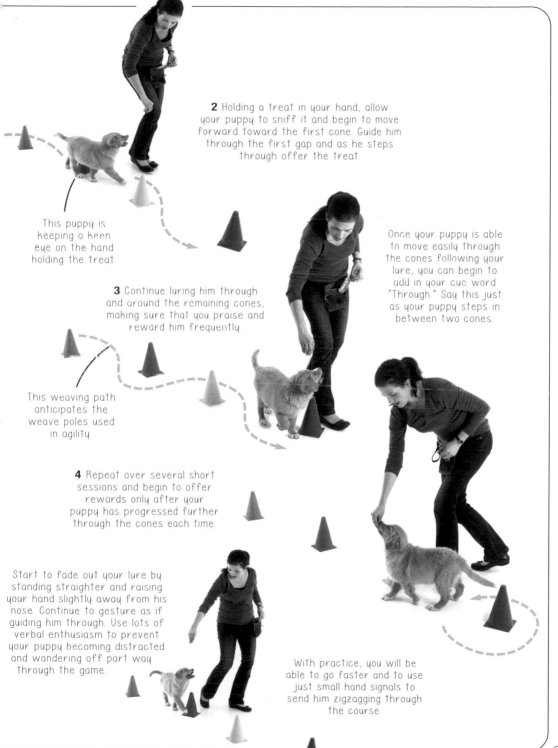

2 Holding a treat in your hand, allow your puppy to sniff it and begin to move forward toward the first cone. Guide him through the first gap and as he steps through offer the treat.

This puppy is keeping a keen eye on the hand holding the treat

Once your puppy is able to move easily through the cones following your lure, you can begin to add in your cue word "Through." Say this just as your puppy steps in between two cones.

3 Continue luring him through and around the remaining cones, making sure that you praise and reward him frequently

This weaving path anticipates the weave poles used in agility

4 Repeat over several short sessions and begin to offer rewards only after your puppy has progressed further through the cones each time.

Start to fade out your lure by standing straighter and raising your hand slightly away from his nose. Continue to gesture as if guiding him through. Use lots of verbal enthusiasm to prevent your puppy becoming distracted and wandering off part way through the game.

With practice, you will be able to go faster and to use just small hand signals to send him zigzagging through the course.

I'LL GIVE YOU A CLUE!

Life Skill Achieved: I can listen and watch carefully.

The aim of this game is to hide a treat or toy in one of a number of pots and then to signal by pointing to the right pot. Your puppy learns the importance of paying attention to you since it will speed up his success rate. Although dogs have evolved an amazing ability to be able to follow our lead when we point, it always helps to practice this technique to reinforce the value of owner and dog working together.

Moving On On walks you can drop a treat or a ball, then, after taking a few steps away, turn and point to it saying "There it is!" This is a great way to get your puppy to focus on searching for the dropped treats, drawing attention away from other distractions. Sniffing the ground is also used as a calming signal to other dogs and so it is a very useful way to encourage your puppy to send "I'm no threat" messages.

Place two pots on the floor, right side up.

1 If your puppy can already "Stay" in one place, you can position him a short distance away from the pots. Otherwise, it may be easier to ask another family member to gently hold him so that he can see what you are doing.

STANDING TALL
If you have been crouching, practice while standing up. Try taking a few steps away from the pots before pointing.

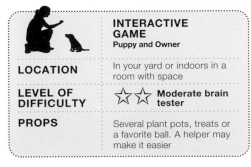

	INTERACTIVE GAME Puppy and Owner
LOCATION	In your yard or indoors in a room with space
LEVEL OF DIFFICULTY	☆☆ **Moderate brain tester**
PROPS	Several plant pots, treats or a favorite ball. A helper may make it easier

2 Show your puppy the treat or the toy and then place it in one of the pots. Pause, waiting for your puppy to look directly at you and then point to this pot just as your helper releases your puppy.

3 Repeat this game, placing the toy into either pot randomly before pointing to it. Make sure that your puppy looks at you before you point so that he is definitely seeing your signal and not just going to the pot he saw you place the toy inside.

Introduce your verbal cue "There!" as you point to the pot containing the toy or treat.

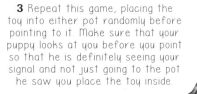

4 Give enthusiastic praise when your puppy finds the treat or toy in the pot in which you have hidden it.

1 The next stage is to place the toy in the pot while your puppy is distracted or out of the room. Now he will be entirely reliant on your signal. Stand back, wait for him to look at you before pointing to the correct pot, at which point your helper can release him.

2 Once your puppy has got the idea of the game and is responding well to your signal, you can begin to add in extra pots. Do this slowly so that he is not confused by the choice.

SNAKES AND LADDERS

Life Skill Achieved: I have great balance and coordination.

There are many ways to create an exciting obstacle course in your yard for your puppy's enjoyment. This game brings two examples together in a simple precursor to future agility games, helping your puppy become used to moving over and through props and being aware of his own movements.

	INTERACTIVE GAME Puppy and Owner
LOCATION	In the yard preferably with few distractions
LEVEL OF DIFFICULTY	☆ **Easy brain game**
PROPS	A play tunnel, a ladder (or a set of canes) and some treats

Snake: Zooming through the tunnel is a game that your puppy can start very early. Some tiny puppies will fit perfectly through a cat tunnel but, for practical purposes, a children's play tunnel is ideal.

1 Begin with the tunnel folded up so it appears like a hoop. Lure your puppy through using a treat and praise, and then tempt him back the other way.

Ladder: If you are using a proper ladder, this should be placed flat on the ground. If using canes, place them on the ground as if they were ladder rungs, with enough space between so that your puppy can step over them. Initially just lay them flat on the ground so that the puppy can get used to walking over them without worrying that his feet will strike one of them. Once he is confident moving between the canes on the ground, you can raise them up a little and add some extra "rungs" to the ladder.

1 Encourage your puppy to walk over the rungs, praising his attempts at stepping over.

3 Once he s confident, ou can open the tunnel completely.

4 Toss some treats or a favorite toy inside it. Allow your puppy time to explore the tunnel.

5 If he enters at one end, encourage him to go through and exit through the other end.

If he is slow to walk down the tunnel, try moving to the other end and attempt to lure him through with a treat.

2 When he is confident in stepping through it, allow a small section to open up and repeat the lesson.

He's through! The treat does the trick.

Moving On Once your puppy has learned both components, you can combine them so that after tackling the ladder, he can zoom through the snake. This can be added to other obstacle activities such as "Walk The Plank" and "In and Out and Round About" for added interest.

2 Try to keep your puppy's attention focused on you and the treat that you are holding to encourage him over the rungs of the ladder.

3 Once he has got used to it, you can raise the canes on little flowerpot saucers to make a course over which he can trot and run.

SPLISH-SPLASH

Life Skill Achieved: I am relaxed and confident.

Introducing your puppy to water early on can benefit him in many ways. Firstly, it adds an extra form of stimulus that your puppy can learn to tolerate; this makes it easier to walk him or to encourage him into the yard when it's wet outside. De-sensitizing a puppy to water in a careful way can help some dogs to tolerate bathing and any future swimming exercise with greater patience.

1 Prepare your tray or basin in a safe place and add a small amount of tepid water.

2 Encourage your puppy to explore. This may involve sitting on the other side and encouraging him to approach and step in, or by placing a toy or treats in the water.

3 Praise your puppy for stepping into the water. Steady your puppy as he jumps in. You may need to keep it very shallow at first and then, over a few play sessions, gradually top it up so that your puppy can happily splish-splash around even more.

	INTERACTIVE GAME Puppy and Owner
LOCATION	Outside, although this can be done indoors on a tiled or stone floor that is resilient to some water spillage
LEVEL OF DIFFICULTY	☆ **Easy brain exercise**
PROPS	A large, shallow tray or basin, towels or spare puppy pee-pads, some tepid water in a bucket. A towel for drying off

Use a treat to reward your puppy if he will sit or stand placidly in the water.

4 Puppies can get cold very quickly so keep water play brief and make sure that he is dried off thoroughly afterward.

5 Play the "Spin-Spin" game on a towel to help to dry his feet afterward

Make sure that you dry him well after this game. This also is good training for getting him used to being handled.

Moving On As your puppy matures physically and his physical ability improves, you may wish to encourage him to swim or play in a paddling pool in your yard. Caution should always be taken around water, however, as so many potential hazards exist. Add in extra control around water by practicing getting your puppy to "Sit" and wait before you give the go-ahead to jump into the water. You should also practice calling him away from the fun (remembering to praise and reward him well when he complies and comes to you) so that you have better control at a later date when he is having a lot of fun at the park. Being able to call your puppy away from something he is enjoying is a useful lesson for many situations.

SURF PUP

Life Skill Achieved: I have great balance and coordination.

This is a game for puppies that adore playing in water. It is best kept for warmer weather and is meant for playing in an easily monitored paddling pool rather than any open body of water. This game takes your "Step Up" and "Yoga Dog" games to a new dimension. Using the same principles, your puppy can practice balancing his front feet on the swim float. Not all puppies will enjoy water games and so you must observe your puppy at all times and make sure that you never do more than he is happy with.

Your puppy must be comfortable playing games in water before starting this lesson.

Moving On You will be able to increase the depth of the water in the paddling pool very slowly over time, and if your puppy enjoys himself and feels sufficiently confident, he may even try to climb on the float. However, this is meant to be a fun yard game and any activity in deeper moving water is not considered safe for puppies. There are water sports that can be enjoyed by keen swimmers, and of course local swimming areas where adult dogs can safely play.

1 The paddling pool should contain no more than a couple of inches of water to start with; if less is needed to keep your puppy comfortable then this is entirely acceptable.

	INTERACTIVE GAME Puppy and Owner
LOCATION	Outside in your yard
LEVEL OF DIFFICULTY	☆☆☆☆ Advanced brain game
PROPS	A shallow paddling pool, a swim float, water, treats and a dry towel

Don't rush this game as your puppy will be dealing with many unfamiliar sensations.

2 Place the swim float in the paddling pool and allow your puppy to enter the water to sniff and investigate. Offer lots of praise while he does so.

3 Next, lure your puppy to step onto the float with his front feet. Use a treat held to his nose to encourage him to step forward. Initially he may only use one foot but you should be prepared to release the treat as soon as it touches the float. By using only a tiny amount of water to begin with, the float should not move about too much at this stage.

With practice your puppy should be able to learn to stand in the water with his front feet on the float.

4 Repeat the exercise to encourage your puppy to begin stepping onto the float. Take your time and use enticing treats. The float will be wobbly and this can take some getting used to.

5 Remember to take regular breaks and to keep your puppy dry and warm when he gets out of the water.

Introduce your verbal cue "Surf" as he steps onto the float. With practice, this will become your signal to start the game.

WALK THE PLANK

Life Skill Achieved: I have great balance and coordination.

This pirate-themed game can be lots of fun and be quite simply adapted to suit your puppy's size, age, confidence level and natural instincts.

	INTERACTIVE GAME **Puppy and Owner**
LOCATION	In your yard
LEVEL OF DIFFICULTY	☆ **Easy brain exercise**
PROPS	A wooden board, treats

1 Lie the plank on the ground where it is stable and unlikely to wobble.

Encourage your puppy to one end of it and, using a food lure, guide him to step onto the plank. The idea is to get your puppy to put all four feet on the plank and then to walk along it from one end to the other.

HIDE AND SEEK

Life Skill Achieved: I can have freedom.

Increase your puppy's inclination to come running when you call and to keep an eye on you during walks, by playing this traditional game where you hide and your puppy seeks.

	INTERACTIVE GAME **Puppy and Owner**
LOCATION	In your home, yard and on walks
LEVEL OF DIFFICULTY	☆ ☆ **Moderate brain tester**
PROPS	No props needed although rewards are always helpful when playing games

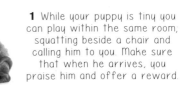

1 While your puppy is tiny you can play within the same room; squatting beside a chair and calling him to you. Make sure that when he arrives, you praise him and offer a reward.

2 The aim is for him to walk the length of the plank without stepping off.

3 Confident puppies may even feel happy to take the plunge into a pool of water.

Moving On If your puppy loves water and is confident playing water games, then he may enjoy actually stepping into a paddling pool placed at the end of the plank. Make sure that you practice teaching him to wait at the end of the plank for you to give your "Go ahead" signal. This will improve your control around other water. Always supervise your puppy if you are playing with water. Never leave him alone around a filled pool or pond and always make sure that he is dried off thoroughly afterward.

It is fine to offer help by calling to him until he finds you

3 As he matures and you progress with your Sit/Stay, you can get him to sit in place while you move further away. It can be helpful to have another family member gently restrain him if he insists on following you while you try to hide.

2 Start to play the game by ducking out of sight while he is distracted. Wait for a moment and then call him. Hopefully he will come searching for you.

Moving On While on walks, you can step behind trees while your puppy is distracted. Keep an eye on where he is and help him to find you by whistling or chirping to draw his attention to you if he struggles.

When he is ready, you can start to play the game outside. Puppies can struggle if they see you leave them, so don't push if your puppy isn't ready. To minimize stress, he should be called to find you almost as soon as you are out of sight.

SOCCER FANATIC

Life Skill Achieved: I am fun to spend time with!

Puppies can have an awful lot of fun with large soccer balls. This game can be as simple or complex as needed to suit your puppy. While your puppy is very small, most soccer balls will work for this game. However, as he grows, you may need to find tougher types of ball to prevent him from puncturing it too often. Large, tough balls are available although many dogs will be perfectly happy playing with slightly deflated balls, which enables them to get hold of the ball more easily in their mouths.

The key to this game is to break up the components into small parts and move on only when your puppy is very confident and succeeding at the stage which you are practicing.

1 Build your puppy's interest in the game by praising and rewarding him each time he shows an interest in the ball.

Some puppies are naturally drawn to balls while others need some encouragement. Rolling it from side to side with a hand or foot can increase his interest.

Moving On If you would like to introduce a goal, then start the next game directly in front of your chosen goal posts. As he nudges at the ball, you can let it go so that it rolls into the goal. Immediately praise him and reward him well. Repeat the sessions and focus on teaching him that pushing the ball through the goal posts is what brings the rewards. Gradually move him further away from the goal and always respond with excitement and praise when he gets it right.

INTERACTIVE GAME Puppy and Owner	
LOCATION	In your yard, or inside if breakables are removed from the area of play
LEVEL OF DIFFICULTY	☆☆☆☆☆ **Advanced brain game**
PROPS	A soccer ball, goal posts

3 Begin to wait until he specifically nudges the lower half of the ball since this will make moving it much easier and more efficient. Reward him every time he gets this right.

2 Next, you need to increase the likelihood of your puppy actually making contact with the ball. Wait until he nudges the soccer ball with his nose (or paws at it) before you praise and reward him. At this stage keep hold of the ball and remove it when the session is over.

4 Once he is touching the ball reliably, you can start to build up to harder pushes by withholding the praise and reward unless the ball actually moves. Loosen your grip on the ball so that it can move slightly each time.

2 The aim is for your puppy to nudge or paw the ball between the posts to score a goal. You want to deliver your praise and a reward when the ball actually rolls into the goal, so that your puppy gets to realize that scoring the goal brings the prize.

1 Adding a couple of goal posts in the shape of cones or empty flower pots introduces an extra element of fun into the game.

ACKNOWLEDGMENTS

Many thanks to all the owners, colleagues and friends who have given their suggestions about the games they love to play with their puppies; I wish I could have fitted them all in. I would like to thank all the owners and their puppies for their help with the photoshoot which is always such fun: specifically thank you to Tracey Eve, Kim Miles, Ann Moon, Sarah Morling, Robert Stuhldreer, Naguib Thabet, Ian and Diane Thompson, and Jackie Weyman. Once again, thanks to the editor and publishers for allowing me this exciting opportunity to write about one of my favorite subjects, and to Ruth for yet again volunteering to proofread. Finally, to Cohen who constantly reminds me of the importance of play in everyday life.

PICTURE CREDITS